T0158806

Management
for You

Management
for You
Leadership Can Be
Color-Blind

Author of Managing in Black and White

Ellen E. Grant

MANAGEMENT
LEADERSHIP CAN BE COLOR-BLIND

iUniverse books may be ordered through booksellers or by contacting:

iUniverse
1663 Liberty Drive
Bloomington, IN 47403
www.iuniverse.com
1-800-Authors (1-800-288-4677)

Because of the dynamic nature of the Internet, any web addresses or links contained in this book may have changed since publication and may no longer be valid. The views expressed in this work are solely those of the author and do not necessarily reflect the views of the publisher, and the publisher hereby disclaims any responsibility for them.

Any people depicted in stock imagery provided by Thinkstock are models, and such images are being used for illustrative purposes only. Certain stock imagery © Thinkstock.

ISBN: 978-1-5320-0254-0 (sc)
ISBN: 978-1-5320-0246-5 (e)

Library of Congress Control Number: 2016911431

Print information available on the last page.

iUniverse rev. date: 04/27/2017

Scripture quotations marked KJV are from the Holy Bible, King James Version (Authorized Version). First published in 1611. Quoted from the KJV Classic Reference Bible, Copyright © 1983 by The Zondervan Corporation.

To all those who strive to reach their full
potential in the area of management

CONTENTS

PREFACE

All things are possible to him that believes.

—Mark 9:23

This book is a follow-up to *Managing in Black & White*, which I wrote in 1991. My goal was to use my experience as a manager to assist new women managers of color through the occasional minefield. Through many happy and sad experiences while working on various degrees, all the way to my determination to secure a PhD, I learned through asserting myself to be recognized as competent enough to be promoted into management roles. I assure you I did not skip any steps on the career ladder; I had no family legacy or riches to get into any position I secured. It was a combination of hard work, blessings, and having a mentor who recognized I had something to contribute to any organization—and of knowing the skills needed to be effective in the workplace.

I received positive feedback after publication. That led to articles, radio interviews, small-market TV interviews, as well as mild sales via Amazon. The book was also well received by the local library, which had copies in various branches. Though it did not reach the level of large-scale national attention, I had the satisfaction of knowing I was helping others.

It's certainly a different world now than when I initially ventured to write. Even with a black female secretary of state, CEOs at Xerox Corporation and Sam's Club, an attorney general, secretary of the treasury, and president of a national foundation, our nation still struggles to find the right balance to reflect the diversity of color among female management.

Many of the issues women of color face in advancing in the workplace remain the same as when I first wrote about them in 1991.

- The Bureau of Labor Statistics / US Dept. of Labor reports that the weekly earnings of full-time workers reflect an approximately $200-a-week wage differential between white and black female workers.
- Women overall are still not paid equally to men in too many instances.
- Majority-race managers often choose up-and-comers who look like them to sprinkle the magic fairy dust of advancement on. Women of color sometimes hear of positions and apply, only to hear through the grapevine the "die is cast," meaning someone has already been deemed the chosen one. Higher management is merely going through the motions of having others apply, lest there be legal equal-opportunity consequences.
- Opportunities to engage with others outside the office—on the golf course and other social venues—exclude women and those of color, leading to a two-tiered system of advancement in the workplace.

Minicuts, as I call them, include not being given visible assignments to demonstrate competency; relevant comments in high-level meetings are ignored or mimicked by another from the majority and accepted. When a woman of color delivers her thoughts assertively, stereotypes persist, such as the one assigned to First Lady Michelle Obama as "an angry black woman."

I do know I have "succeeded" in the eyes of many, always through the mercy and grace of God. In spite of my missteps, failures, and faults, I remain with servant leadership at my core.

The goal for this book is to help you succeed with your business goals. My experiences as a professional black woman might point the way for others, regardless of color. I can provide direction for those of you who are determined to achieve your greatest potential and to thereby attain the highest salary, the loftiest position, and the widest recognition of which you are capable.

The key to reaching your goal is learning how to market yourself, and that is what this book will teach you how to do. It is a basic premise of marketing that you must have a product that someone else wants. In management, the "product" can be certain skills, specific types of experience, perhaps a feel for situations and people, and an eye for color and design. Essentially, the product is you.

To ensure that you deal from a position of strength and that you do not sell yourself short, you should deepen your understanding of the four main areas covered by this book:

1) Where We're Coming From: a historical perspective on the black woman in the workforce

2) Where You Intend to Go: a discussion of how to build a professional image with innovation, market analysis, and market positioning

3) What to Do When You Get There: direction on how to deal with your superiors, subordinates, and peers

4) How to Go Above and Beyond: some to-the-point insider information on management issues ranging from communication to mentoring

At the conclusion of this book is an appendix with examples of employee scenarios and suggestions for intervention.

PART I

Where We're Coming From

The history of black women in the workforce, environmental
factors, roadblocks to equality, and equal opportunity
are all part of where we've come from. Looking at where
we were can help us decide where we need to go.

History of Black Women Workers

To plot a true and steady course for your destination, it is always wise to know where you are now and how you got there. That is why a brief retrospective view of the status of black women as workers is in order. I will not deal here with the history of black women prior to 1970. Such scholars as Frances Beal, Paula Giddings, and Angela Davis have already documented the earlier periods of our history well, and their work should be consulted directly.

The numbers continue to tell the story. As of December 4, 2015 (Report 15-2292), according to the Bureau of Labor Statistics / US Department of Labor, the percentage of all women in the workplace was 6.1 percent. For white women in the workplace, unemployment was 4 percent. For black women in America, that figure in 2014 was 8 percent.

If, as the figures show, we black women are picking up the slack and becoming the major breadwinners, why do our wages still not equal those of white women? The Bureau of Labor Statistics / US Dept. of Labor's December 2014 Report 1051 states, "Between 1979 and 2013, inflation-adjusted earnings (also called constant-dollar earnings) rose by 31 percent for White women, compared with an increase of 20 percent for Black women and 15 percent for Hispanic women."

Unfortunately, some women face a double hurdle when they are black or Hispanic in a majority white society because they are females in a male-dominated society.

Roadblocks to Equality

Certainly roadblocks to equality in the workplace challenge black women, and women in general, with the goal of earning equal pay.

Despite the effort expended on behalf of federal comparable-pay-for-comparable-work legislation, it remains stymied by lawmakers (most of them male), even though fully supported by the president.

As for getting a foot in the door of the executive suite, women today still face discrimination because of their gender. Arranging a working lunch or dinner may be misconstrued or not readily accepted when offered to a male work colleague. A woman may have a much harder time than her male counterpart does finding a mentor, someone at a higher level interested in helping her career along.

Catalyst's report "People of Color in Management" reveals that 41.7 percent are white women compared to 5.4 percent black women[1].

As I stated earlier, the black woman must counter these difficulties, and more beside, given the double jeopardy of sexism and racism.

Certain other variables also hamper a black woman's career aspirations. United States Health and Human Services statistics confirm that blacks have shorter life spans than whites. "Life expectancy for black females was 3.3 years lower than that of white females. This difference was due to higher death rates for black females for heart disease, cancer, diabetes, prenatal conditions, and stroke."

The black teen unemployment rate is higher than for white teens, and the expectations of society influence the black female's ability to take her rightful place in the workforce. For the time being, I can only urge the majority society to narrow the wage gap and to provide us with a level playing field that will help us compete on an equal footing. Obviously, we must continue to help ourselves and our sisters, and that is what the rest of this book is all about.

Equal Opportunity

I would like to take this opportunity to recognize the Civil Rights Act of 1964. This bill, I feel, only included women because the general consensus was that this inclusion would undermine the bill. Fortunately

---

[1] Source: Current Population Survey, Bureau of Labor Statistics, "Table 1: Employed and Experienced Unemployed Persons by Detailed Occupation, Sex, Race, and Hispanic or Latino Ethnicity, 2012," Annual Averages 2012, Unpublished Tabulations (2013).

for women, minorities, and the handicapped, that plan backfired. The bill began a foundation for looking at all levels of rights for women, minorities, and the handicapped. It has to be renewed every twenty-five years. A colleague reminded me that this bill came up again for passage in 1999.

These laws legislate equal opportunity, but they do not and cannot legislate equal access to that opportunity. For example, saying that women cannot be kept out of carpeted Corporate America doesn't mean we'll get in or stay in. Episodes like Anita Hill, Judge Sol Wachtler, and Senator Packwood are only the tip of the iceberg, because they're celebrities. In fact, there's a continuing backlash out there.

Look in the business section of almost any big-city newspaper where pictures of those promoted are placed. I would bet that the majority of those on that page are white men, then white women. Many wonder why, as the Catalyst Organization cites in a 1997 *Wall Street Journal* article, 2 percent of senior executives at the largest corporations are women: Are people really afraid that this mere 2 percent will rule the world? Some facts from a *Buffalo News* 1996 article: "Federal Bureau of Labor statistics say white men make up 41 percent of the workforce but hold 90 percent of the senior ranks of all occupations."

Gender diversity actually works. The push to get more females at the top isn't just about women's rights. The best case for bringing gender diversity into the C-Suite is made by cold, hard cash.

Companies with a high representation of women board members significantly outperformed those with no female directors, according to a 2011 *Catalyst* analysis of financial results at Fortune 500 companies.

Even same-sex couples appear to be getting more attention to their needs than persons of color. In June 2000, it was announced that three large car manufacturers would pay for medical coverage for those in a same-sex relationship. This is still a milestone, because it means that the world can recognize that there are differences in people, that differences do not mean less qualified or willing to work and can be assets to an organization. Indeed there are differences, but differences can and should be embraced and celebrated.

Environmental Factors

Environmental factors affect how well we may achieve our potential. Below, I've listed five main areas that I feel affect advancement. Ask yourself what environmental factors have occurred or are in play now that are impacting your organization.

1. **General wealth of the country**
    Due to the consistent good news in stock market and lower unemployment rate for the general populace, many companies may not feel pressured to reach out to underrepresented populations. Keep in mind that the current unemployment rate does not include those who have given up looking for work.

2. **Computer technology affects staffing**
    The development of computers and technology and the accompanying technology is proliferating so rapidly that job vacancies for a population of skilled workers cannot keep up with job demands.

3. **The new employee is recruited**
    Employees are being recruited from Canada, Russia, and China to fill positions in the computer technology field. This infusion of "new employees," while helpful to the organizational bottom line, can often lead to cultural disequilibrium. For example, the new employee who doesn't speak English may converse with his/her peers on work assignments using his native language. This can often lead to the English-speaking member of the team feeling "left out" or concerned that secrets are being shared.

4. **Education gap**
    American culture is proceeding along a continuum; there is a larger gap between those with a college degree and those without

one. There are a number of positions seeking either a college degree or technological expertise. At the same time, the number of people available for service positions appears to be on the rise. People who will serve us in restaurants, clean hotels, or mow lawns are not readily available to fill such positions as evidenced by the want ads seeking these types of workers.

5. **Part-time employees.**

The number of persons employed part-time for economic reasons (sometimes referred to as involuntary part-time workers) was little changed at 6.0 million in December, down by 764,000 over the year. These individuals, who would have preferred full-time employment, were working part-time because their hours had been cut back or because they were unable to find full-time jobs (Bureau of Labor Statistics, January 8, 2016). A number of factors contribute to the desire of both employers and potential employees to choose to work in a part-time environment. First, it is less expensive for employers to not have to pay the cost of benefits like medical insurance and holiday pay. On the other hand, there are people who want and/or need a flexible schedule. They may have children or other family members in need of care. They themselves may be in college or other training programs, be semiretired, or just desire more free time.

Conclusion

In summary, yes, it's a hard struggle. Many employees are now demanding that newly hired employees be proven to be as qualified as they are, or the employer will be taken to court on reverse discrimination charges by the current workers. Even though we know that often women and men of color have to have twice as many qualifications to even get into the interview, women and men of color will continue to be challenged. Also, just because we get the job doesn't mean women of color will be paid the same. The Catalyst Organization reported in a 1997 *Wall Street Journal* article that for every dollar white male managers earned, white women earned fifty-nine cents and minority women fifty-seven cents.

It is my hope that companies will finally realize that racism and sexism are costly. Continuing these patterns can cause reduced employee productivity as a result of low employee morale and increased use of sick days from depression or stress that occurs from poor working conditions. I witnessed this over and over as a clinical therapist who worked with clients with such work issues.

I remember working in a beginning supervisory position and being told I didn't have enough experience. So I worked two full-time jobs in the mental health field while I finished the last one and one-half years of graduate school and started my doctorate degree.

Because of this experience, I feel that I can speak very well to the "overqualified" and "stress" factors, but I'm nostalgic about the hard bones my grandmother said I'd have to sometimes chew. Success, like in a prize fight, is getting up one more time after you've been knocked down. One more point: remember that Ginger Rogers had to dance backward when dancing with Fred Astaire!

Companies will not be successful in the long term if they have a credibility issue in getting their employees to truly believe they are out to embrace their employees' comprehensive well-being in the workplace. A win for employees and a win for the company should be the mission in the corporate suite. Companies that have sexual, racial, and ethnic diversity are reflective of the consumer market where women make many decisions in the home. If companies want to gain in the marketplace, their own workforce must reflect this diversity.

Part 2

Where You Intend to Go

If you have read this far, you have obviously accepted my challenge to head straight for the top. As you will see, getting there can be, will be, an uphill effort, but it can also be half the satisfaction and more than half the fun. Determining where you want to go is the first step to achieving something. It has several components, and in this chapter, I focus on the ones I've found most useful. You have to consider how you present yourself, what you and others really want, and tap into your gifts as a female leader.

Successful Marketing

The image you present to the professional world is, if not everything, a significant factor in your quest for success. You will need, therefore, to step outside yourself and take an objective look at what others see. Imagine that you and your competitors for the upper reaches of management are products arrayed on a shelf. Which would you choose? More to the point, which would senior management choose?

By following some basic principles for positioning yourself in the best light, you can tip the scales in your favor to ensure you're in the best place at the right time to bring the company enhanced value.

You need to be watchful for younger subordinates eager to topple you from your position, and you will need, as well, to continue to pursue professional excellence that will keep you ahead of the pack. Here are some suggestions to stay current.

- Are you honing your skills in your field to the best of your ability?
- Have you taken care to become visibly involved in community groups? Volunteering to serve on boards and to speak on behalf of respected organizations will help establish you as a leader.
- Are you taking care of you, your most important product, with regular exercise, good nutrition, and good health habits? Is your physical and mental health up to the stresses inherent in success?
- Do you know when to fight and when to flee (good timing)? Can you judge the golden opportunity to let the decision-makers know you are interested in a position of greater responsibility and the time to let your actions speak for you?
- Are you alert to competitors who might appropriate and take credit for your ideas, realizing in advance that competitors could affect your potential by imitation and making allowance for such an

effect? Do you take care, before presenting an idea at a meeting, to put it in writing?

- Do you seek continuing education and stay abreast of the literature in your field, continuing to seek further innovations? Are you computer-literate even if computers aren't the main focus of your career?

As your career matures and you achieve your niche, there are additional steps you can take to maintain your position. For example, take care to keep your superior informed of your achievements in and out of the office. Both your professional milestones and your community activities will demonstrate that your career and the image of your organization take high priority in your personal scheme of things. Along the same lines, you should consider writing for professional journals in your field, and see to it that your boss and the local media receive copies of published work. Whether writing is your forte or not, volunteering at the office to work on projects of special interest to you—even when this means taking on extra work—will always be favorably noticed.

Mentor Board

While you work to shape your talents to the corporate mold and to show yourself to be an enthusiastic team player, you must also be aware that as a woman and especially woman of color, you may need to furnish your own cheering section. I have strongly advised those I've coached to form what I describe as a "mentor board." That is, select a small group of advisers you admire who can give you feedback on issues of concern to you. You would be wise not to choose your entire board from the same profession and/or culture as your own. Allow this learning opportunity to flourish. It can only do so if it generates the diversity of thought that can only come from voices different from your own. As you move through your professional career, changes in location, jobs, and time availability may cause a natural progression in mentor-board membership. My present mentor board consists of a retired black female corporate manager; a white, middle-age male corporate president; a retired black male university professor; (my parents, my Aunt Jane, all deceased, but their principles remain with me); a white female partner in a law firm, and a white banker. Although three members of my board have remained throughout my work career, the make-up of my mentor board is not the same as it was ten years ago. (There's more about mentoring in part 4.)

You should also choose a mentor within your organization to help you get to where you want to go. If you've done your homework you will know who calls the shots in your organization. You will make it your business—literally—to forge an alliance with one of them. If you can do so, you gain both a "friend at court" who is willing to cut red tape for you and a certain amount of power-by-association.

In this type of relationship, the senior executive acts as your mentor, taking you under his or her wing and guiding you up the corporate ladder. Ironically, a black woman, for all her visibility when her firm wants to showcase its dedication to equal opportunity, is often overlooked by would-be mentors. There are ways around this shortsightedness, however.

I recommend that you choose a "silent mentor," someone in top management you admire. Observe this person carefully and adopt as your own those mannerisms, expressions, and ways of approaching a problem that match your personal style. (Be wary, however, of becoming so slavish in your imitation of your mentor that you become a caricature.) If yours is an organization where senior managers practice (or claim to practice) an open-door policy, ask your mentor for career advice—that's always flattering. Send him or her copies of articles you have written for publication. Let the manager know you are interested in taking on increased responsibilities and sound him or her out about opportunities that exist under his or her aegis. In dealing with your mentor, you will need to walk a fine line, as I have mentioned before, remaining friendly and admiring but always professional. You should not, for example, expect to lunch or socialize together after work.

Mind Adjustment

From a psychological perspective, women sometimes do have personal issues that may impede their ability to move forward. For example:

Low self-esteem and self-blame are ego processes that can determine a woman's ability to believe in herself. Women have been socialized to be caretakers, to be needed, to bake bread and make babies. Many of us go through a stage of ego reassessment, determining who we are, and sometimes it may seem we women are responsible for the bad things that happen. You know the "blame the victim" scenario: "It's her fault she didn't get the job—she didn't prepare" and so forth. In fact, it's often society's problem that women still aren't viewed as equal partners. We need to turn our strengths that we as women have—compassion, women's intuition, and what I call *facho*, which equals assertiveness plus sensitivity plus team spirit—into a marketable commodity or value that can guide us to success.

Another important fact is intertwined in our **speaking and listening skills**. Women are often more intimidated in meetings and have a tendency to talk too low or too fast and mumble. The latter happens perhaps because they feel the men aren't going to pay attention. Women's Miss Manners–style of speaking—"If I listen to you nicely, you'll listen to me nicely"—is often a disservice to us. In fact, some men and women just jump in forcefully when they have something to say. You can overcome this by speaking forcefully and slowly. Make your major point first and then expand on it. Never open with "This may not be on point about what we've been saying, but ..." This will weaken your credibility for the rest of the meeting and perhaps into the future.

How you present yourself, how you want to be viewed as the ultimate professional, is yours to design. If you're not fully confident, watch and listen to other professionals you respect. Do this not to mimic or copy their behavior but to observe their best and see how you can use it with your own style to be your authentic self.

How You Manage Others

In the all-important undertaking of image-building, how you manage yourself professionally is only one aspect. Another, equally important, is how you manage others. To do so successfully, you must begin with an understanding of what makes people tick. According to psychologist Abraham Maslow, there are five basic human needs, common to all of us:

- We need to satisfy our physical requirements for food, air, water, and so on.
- We need to fulfill ourselves; that is, live up to our capabilities.
- We need to feel a sense of personal worth; that is, to feel important and valuable.
- We need to feel that we belong, that we are part of an accepting group.
- We need to feel safe, both physically and emotionally.

Toward a Psychology of Being, an early work by Maslow published in 1962, emphasized the then-basic needs. In today's workplace, many of the needs are still there. People want to have jobs that let them experience fulfillment and feel a sense of personal worth. We all have the desire to be recognized for doing a good job. People can't experience fulfillment without a positive environment, and the manager is the one who sets the tone for the environment.

Are you basically a distrustful-type manager who believes that all subordinates are lazy and require tight control, rules with an iron fist, and delights in seeing that rules are followed to the letter? You would accept that workers are motivated by physiological needs but would be likely to ignore the other four needs.

A simple example is Mr. Murray Wilson, who criticized Amelia Clark, who delayed getting the requested report to him by one hour. Ms. Clark's peer, Ms. Smith, had a family medical emergency and thus was not able to do the required graphics for Mr. Wilson's report. Although

Ms. Clark advised Mr. Wilson of the delay, all Mr. Wilson could see was that Ms. Clark was late in getting the report to him, not the unforeseen circumstances that necessitated some flexibility on Mr. Wilson's part, showing a more relaxed style of management. A manager with strong self-confidence will also be a more compassionate manager who cares about the overall well-being of his or her employees.

The manager with strong self-confidence recognizes that people are driven by more than the most basic needs and treats them accordingly. He or she views management as the art of balancing the needs of the organization and the employees and has a knack for eliciting the best work of which the staff is capable. This manager realizes that to earn respect, one must give respect. This does not mean that he or she is an ineffectual disciplinarian—all the better, more likely, for being sensitive and understanding.

In the previous example, if Mr. Wilson had more freely embraced a more relaxed style of management, he would have understood that Ms. Smith's unexpected absence could not have been foreseen. He would have been more understanding of Ms. Clark's delay in submitting the report to him.

So far our discussion of image has been gender-neutral and could apply equally to men and women. We would do ourselves a disservice, however, if we neglected to consider certain aspects of our social and cultural shaping as women that can work to our advantage as managers. Heaven knows we have enough difficulties to overcome when we finally achieve a position of authority that we cannot afford to overlook a potentially profitable trait.

Strengths Innate to Women

One of these aspects is intuition. I also call it "mother wit"—sensitivity to others' feelings, coupled with the ability to interpret the emotions behind the words and the real meaning of body language. It is the valuable—and in a managerial way, useful—talent for knowing when emotional crises in the workplace are symptoms of something else.

It was once considered the mark of the up-and-coming executive, black or white, to be "macho"—an exaggerated masculine stereotype, highly aggressive, insensitive to others' feelings, competitive to the point of rancor, given to boorish manners and foul language. These days, macho is out, and what I call "facho"—a blend of assertiveness, sensitivity, and team spirit—is in. Now that the advantage is on our side, shouldn't we use it? We certainly should. The third attribute, being a team player, often comes late to women. Little boys learn about working with their teammates to reach a common goal when they get their first baseball glove and bat. Little girls, sitting on the sidelines and competing for the attention of the cute first baseman, may never learn it at all. But they will have to if they aspire to more than entry-level management.

These innate strengths can often be used to decide on a position or move you're considering in your career. Of course, you will still need to do your homework by researching the position you're reviewing and strength you bring to the role, how you add value, and what challenges you may face in doing so.

Building your image as a team player begins with schooling yourself in the niceties of your organization's corporate culture: its style and code of conduct and the way its business is done. Since men can often rely on the "old-boy network" to set them straight on what is and is not done, you may have to exert extra effort and become super-observant to compete on equal footing. You may also have to curb a degree of individuality. A cornrow hairdo or purple hair and a locker room vocabulary are decided drawbacks in a firm where conservative hairstyles and circumspect language are the norm. For example, if you'd had the opportunity to join IBM a number of years ago, you would have seen all male managers garbed in the corporate uniform, a blue suit and white shirt. Had you attained the ranks of management yourself, you can be sure that you would have worn a blue suit and a white blouse.

The Female Executive's Thirteen Commandments

(Yes, Moses needed only Ten Commandments, but he wasn't dealing with the business world, and he wasn't a woman of color.)

As I said before, you will need high-order skills to advance beyond entry-level management. Identifying mentors, managing others, and being aware of your own strengths are three areas, but there are others. I have summarized those I have found crucial to my own career success.

1. **Set a career goal.** Determine where you want to be professionally three to five years from now and identify what steps it will take to get there, such as further education. Consider whether you can reach your goal in your present organization or field. Based on your current strengths and weaknesses, as well as the competition, will you need to make a change? Assess your priorities. Is a higher salary your main goal? A title? Creative control and satisfaction?

2. **Weave a network of contacts inside and outside your company.** Get to know the managers at your level in every other department; find out who your peers are at other companies in town; join professional organizations—both for women and for practitioners in your field. Don't forget to widen your acquaintances with white men in positions of power men in your profession, particularly. I can vouch for one way to do that. I serve on a volunteer board composed mainly of white male Republicans—quite a coup for a black female Democrat, one that I have turned to my advantage. I make it a point to introduce myself at each monthly meeting to two board members. Eventually I will know them all, will be able to converse with them as a colleague, and will be able to include them among my network of contacts.

3. **Pass it on and give some back.** Someone helped you, so help someone else. Ask them as their "thank you" to help someone else! Remember, you didn't get where you are by yourself—you won't stay there by yourself. Everyone had help to make it.

4. **Become a generalist.** After you have gained expertise in one area of management, such as personnel administration, volunteer to learn about another, such as preparing the department's annual budget. You might also ask to serve on the organization's finance committee or some other in-house task group of interest.

5. **Go the extra mile.** Hard work has never gone out of favor with bosses. Neither has innovation; sometimes a fresh new approach by a fresh new face can solve a long-standing problem.

6. **Learn to manage your time.** This is vital if you hope to achieve a healthy balance between work and play. Discover when you are at peak productivity and tackle your most challenging assignments then. Learn, too, to recognize when you're burning out and when it's time for vacation or a few days off. While you may think you are showing devotion to duty with long hours, your boss will not appreciate it when your work is flawed by stress. Even if you aspire to be Superwoman, force yourself to delegate responsibilities. It enhances your reputation as a team player and gives your staff a change to show what they are capable of doing.

   We can all get plenty of exercise by jumping to conclusions, pushing our luck, and dodging deadlines, but real exercise must be scheduled, just like the next appointment. Being physically fit will enhance and improve your mental alertness, as well as increase your energy level. Part of the physical fitness program includes eating well-balanced meals, taking vitamins, and adopting an exercise program that has your physician's approval.

7. **Become your own public relations person.** There's nothing wrong with distributing an article about yourself to higher-ups. If you do have a revolutionary idea you believe will benefit the company, research it well and put it on paper under your name. Also, don't be afraid to take your revolutionary idea as a risk. Don't be afraid of failure. It helps you maintain readiness for success and makes you stronger and willing to take more risks. Let your

supervisors know about your accomplishments in and out of the office. Take a course in public speaking and then volunteer to practice your new skill on behalf of the company. When you get a bright idea, even if it's not in your primary area of responsibility, outline it in a memo to your boss and to the boss's boss. Share news of your achievements with your staff as well. It will bolster their regard for you and the pride they take in working in your department.

8. **Use criticism to your advantage.** While no one enjoys being made to realize that she is not perfect, no one is perfect—and so you should regard feedback as a learning experience. Weigh the criticism objectively, consider its merit, and take steps to correct your shortcomings. If you can't correct them all, you'll at least get an A for effort.

9. **Assert yourself—nicely.** These days, no woman in the workforce has to roll over and play dead for anyone. By all means, be self-effacing early in the game until you know what the company rules are, but once you do, feel free to put yourself forward a little. Ask relevant questions at meetings or offer a comment based on your experience. When you believe you deserve a raise, go after it, and be prepared to negotiate to get it. I recall an instance when, six months after I assumed a management position, my job description was changed; I was given broader responsibilities and a new title. I asked for a $2,000 raise, which my supervisor turned down. I returned three months later and asked that the raise go into effect the first of the year after my annual performance evaluation. I got the raise. A word of advice: when assertiveness and willingness to negotiate fail to get you what you want, it is time to think about other options. Sometimes you have to move out to move up.

10. **Behave professionally.** Surprise the chauvinists who expect you to rage or cry under pressure. Take a deep breath, and speak slowly and evenly. Remind yourself that there are two sides to every story,

and you might be in the wrong. Your goal is to put things right, and runaway emotions won't accomplish that. Even when you're the injured party, don't give them the satisfaction of seeing that you have been hurt.

11. **Dress professionally.** By that I mean groom and dress yourself in the manner of the highest-ranking female executives in your organization. Unless you are in fashion merchandising, where trendsetting is part of the job description, avoid extremes—no miniskirts, no low-cut dresses, no skin-tight anything, no drop-dead earrings, no flashy colors, no "business" shorts, no matter how well tailored, no cornrows with beads or radical haircuts, no glitzy makeup and nails.

12. **Take risks.** While it can be lonely standing on the brink of a new management position, particularly when you feel all eyes are on you, when you will set your race one hundred years back if you fail, remember that she who hesitates is lost. We need to make and take our own opportunities. When I was in a comfortable middle-management job with the state, I heard about another, more challenging position that would bring me more responsibility, status, and money. During the interview, when asked to state the salary desired, I named a figure $3,000 more than I was already making, thinking that if I didn't get the job, I still had my secure state niche. The interviewer seemed happy with my presentation and my salary expectations and said I would hear shortly. In the meantime, I began to reevaluate my skills and concluded that not only was I well qualified for the position, but I could do the organization a great deal of good. I called back and told the interviewer that I had miscalculated; based on what I had to offer, I was worth $7,000 more than my salary. There was dead silence, and then the interviewer said there were other candidates for the job, and he would have to get back to me. Two days later, he did,

with an offer that matched my higher request. This taught me to take a chance on myself whenever possible.

13. **Be a master of the game**—the game of office politics, that is. If you are going to play office politics, play to win. The basic rule is this: don't make enemies. Even if you don't care for some of your coworkers personally, let the world know that from nine to five, you are a team player. Find out early where the real power of your unit, department, and company lies. This knowledge will help you plot your career path. When you manipulate others—and you will—do so with finesse and for positive reasons. Using or abusing others for your own personal ambitions, while temporarily effective, will eventually be found out. The loss of credibility can damage your career permanently. Never be blatant about your political moves. The smoothest operators are those who are never seen operating. For guidance in this art, observe someone in the upper echelons you admire and see how effortlessly the game is played by a pro. Be a team player so your peers and supervisors know you're concerned about the whole mission of the company, not just your own ego. Your peers may not be women or someone from your profession or race. It's all about developing a relationship with an individual who you believe can teach you something new in the workplace or even on the golf course. It depends on your end goal—to get a promotion or be a better golfer.

PART 3

What to Do When You Get There

This section will address how best to present yourself after you achieve your new role in management. I'll underscore areas of your own personality that hopefully you've already aspired to long before you sought to ascend the management ladder.

Be the Change You Want to See

So many people choose to merely exist instead of live: to not be involved in the call to action to make their life, their environment better for themselves, their families, and/or their neighbors.

One of my favorite quotes is a paraphrase of the African proverb "Many spider webs can tie up a lion." To me, this means collective work, people all working toward a common goal, from a project work team to a neighborhood block club doing street cleaning, all can be successful if they stay focused on making a change together.

Being the change you want to see comes from Mahatma Gandhi's theme that being a successful change agent starts with the individual. Each individual can make it their goal not to whine but to win; not to complain but to conjoin with others to help build a better work environment or humanity.

The values you bring to the workplace influence this change. If you were raised by the Golden Rule—treat everyone with respect as you would like to be treated—you should employ that same ruling in the workplace. I've seen too many people in my career who say they believe in treating all people the same, but then you hear that they told a derogatory joke about women or were overheard saying "Most Muslims are terrorists and shouldn't be given a job with security tasks" at their company. The person who will cheat on their expense account by buying dinner for friends who have no affiliation with work or up-charging taxi expenses is not someone who would show integrity in the workplace in decision making.

Creating positive change requires commitment. I think of the term "follow through" and I also think of the term "commitment," the two in my mind being intrinsically linked. It means that once I take on a task, I am committed to following it through to completion unless it is humanly impossible to do so.

Committing to the task initially should mean that you've given it more than cursory thought. You first draw upon the sincerity of the person who asked you to complete the task. They obviously chose you because you have a value they can align with: you will do the job, commit, and follow through after thorough analyses of whether the work can fit into your tasks at hand.

So many people say yes to a job, take on an assignment, or volunteer without assessing the value of the job within the scope of their entire life. Then instead of bowing out gracefully, they will hang on to the title, be a no-show, often leaving the person who made the request in a very precarious position, vulnerable to a loss of credibility in the eyes of others.

Think on this anonymous quote:

> *Too many people are ready to carry the stool when the piano needs to be moved.*

If you commit to any assignment, make sure you are present, a full participant, by assuming anequal share of the work. Don't be the person who shows up at the eleventh hour of the assignment to do what a person at a lower level of the organization is capable of doing and then wants to take much of the credit or is the first and loudest person at the celebration party. The Golden Rule applies here as well: no one likes to work on a team when the members lack commitment. People will respond when you commit and treat them well.

Management Style

Your name is on the office door. The business cards proclaiming your new title have arrived, and so have you. What now? This is the crucial time when, textbooks and professional journals aside, you have to hunker down and manage people. As you do so, you will begin to develop your own management style.

I have found that a judicious balance of benevolent authoritarianism and a consultative approach that gives employees a voice on some noncritical issues, such as vacation scheduling and changes in work methods, work well in many circumstances. You, of course, will have to decide what works for you in your particular career setting. As always, the buck stops with you, the manager.

The British have a phrase: "Begin as you mean to go on." Here in the United States we speak of "getting off on the right foot," both sage pieces of advice for the fledgling manager. A good beginning is essential to make a budding career blossom. It is particularly important for you as a black woman. You should realize that you will have to work harder to earn the respect of your subordinates than your white or male counterparts. For instance, early on, during the so-called "honeymoon" period when you and your staff are first getting acquainted, don't be lulled into a false sense of security. The abounding sweetness and light may quickly disappear as you begin to act like a boss, setting limits, defining policy, and giving direction and correction where necessary.

Many women are often surprised by the fact that they do have to work harder to sometimes achieve half as much.

Dressing to Manage

People will judge you based on how you appear to them, and the clothing you choose sends a message. The office workplace has become more casual in recent years, but as a person who has been promoted to management and aspires to go higher in the organization, the casual dress codes won't always apply to you. One manager I know never went past the model of a blazer and slacks and/or pantsuit as her idea of a dress-down day at the office. This was certainly in keeping with my belief that one should always dress up. That is, dress up to the next position you hope to achieve. Look at the people who hold positions you aspire to and emulate their manner of professional dress at the office.

Many organizations have instituted dress-down days for their employees. The goals vary, but at least one of these goals is to allow employees the opportunity to have a day of less businesslike attire.

Some companies have orchestrated formally written guidelines about what is acceptable (long pants/khakis) and what is not (cleavage). Other companies align casual days only on specific periods: quarterly, paydays, or to build a charity base. For example, one organization I worked for allowed employees to participate in Dress-Down Fridays only if they paid a dollar. When the pool built to seventy-five dollars, for example; it was donated to a local charity.

Organizations that don't define the guidelines for casual day, however, run the risk of relying on people to police themselves. For the supervisor or manager who wishes to be seen as professional and credible, it is important that she/he dress the part at all times, setting a standard that employees may use as a guideline. There are more suggestions for dress in Office Etiquette in part 4.

Dos and Don'ts When You're Promoted

Do your homework. Before Day One on the job, familiarize yourself with the functions of your department and the people who staff it. Memorize the chain of command, and pay attention as well to the informal networks, or cliques. Unless he or she was promoted within the organization, find out tactfully what happened to your predecessor, with a view to avoiding the same mistakes.

Additional suggestions:

1—Let your staff know right from the start what you expect of them. Meet with them individually to get their opinions on company issues and to ask about their own career aspirations. Make it clear that you respect confidences and that your door is always open.

2—Give praise where it's due. At the same time, don't expect thanks or appreciation yourself, or, worse yet, fish for compliments. If your staff regards you as an egomaniac in need of constant reassurance, you will get neither their respect nor the truth when you need it.

3—Vow that you'll never let them see you sweat, cry, or blow your stack. Justified as these reactions may be in some situations, they are deadly to a woman's career prospects. Unfortunately, too many still believe that pregnant women are emotionally volatile employees whose job performance and commitment suffer because of their condition.

In sum, men and women in the workplace general exhibit styles that are different. Judy Rosener wrote *America's Competitive Secret: Women Managers* and continues to write and lecture on women and male differences in the workplace. In a phone interview this author had with Dr. Rosener in November 2014, she related, "On the continuum, men have more attributes that are quantifiable." "Based on my research I am convinced that the reason women are not promoted (or hired) is due to the fact that organizational policies and practices devalue women because female attributes are difficult to measure and organizations value what they can count" Shouldn't all of Dr. Rosener's quote be in parens?

Office Etiquette

For many of us, Mom and Dad and even Grandma were our first teachers of how to behave at the dinner table. In my family, we knew very soon that horseplay and/or chewing inappropriately would be one of the offenses that would be sure to land us a stint in the basement "prison" to finish our dinner meal in solitary. Unfortunately, no one is usually available to help you with office etiquette in your first real job in the professional arena.

Like using the wrong fork, you may not even realize you're doing the "wrong" thing until perhaps a trusted office colleague mentions that she or he heard someone comment on your offense in the break room. If you don't have a colleague to tell you, you may find yourself passed over for a promotion or not invited on a training program to an exotic resort spot. These nuances in behavior are also part of your supervisor's scorecard for completing your evaluation. Here are a few tips to help you on your way to becoming viewed as professional, as well as articulate, polite, and well mannered.

It's never too late to show the "new and improved you," but it's certainly an added advantage if you can start the new job from day one on the right foot. If you don't feel confident in the area, do some research. Google *etiquette* for a myriad of topics, including using the right silverware, how to introduce colleagues, and so on.

I was enamored by the young English black woman on the national news who commented on her delight at the Queen Mother (Queen Mum) reaching one hundred years of age and the celebration the public participated in. She responded in her high English accent, "She's never set a foot out wrongly!"

1. Please leave makeup preparation at home. It is downright tacky to sit at your desk and apply foundation, eye shadow, and so forth, as well as in the ladies' room. It gives the impression you don't take your job seriously enough to be prepared to work the minute you arrive at the workplace. If you have to set your alarm clock at home fifteen minutes early, then do so.

2. Speaking of makeup, please remember you're going to work, not to the latest hip hop contest. Reserve dramatic style (false eyelashes, overly bright eye shadow, blush, and lipstick) for the evening and weekends, when you can more overtly employ your signature style. The workplace look should be much more subtle. If you're not sure, look at some of the professional magazines you admire and notice the makeup of those in them, or visit your department store's cosmetic department for a makeup consultation.

3. Understated hair styles are the order of the day. Adding purple and burgundy hair swatches is best left for your free time. Hair, even if worn in cornrow fashion, should appear neat and orderly at all times.

4. Never arrive at work with hair rollers in your hair. It is impossible to think you can get people to even think you're well mannered with this behavior. I had a colleague who had a staff member she noticed at eleven in the morning (the employee started at eight) with "bumps under her scarf." Upon closer inspection she noticed this employee was working in a full set of hair rollers. She even had the nerve to cop an attitude and file a grievance with the union steward when she was ordered to go to the ladies room to take them out.

5. If your office has no dress code, then, police yourself. Dressing seductively with a show of cleavage and too much leg or too-tight clothing will get you a derogative nickname and leave you open to more ridicule than you'd prefer. The same with footwear—reserve the platform-type and open-toed sandals for after work.

6. Unkempt and/or dirty fingernails are unbecoming.

7. Off-color jokes likewise. Racial and cultural jokes are (hopefully) obviously discriminating, and telling sexual jokes is likewise unprofessional and distasteful.

8. Learn to use proper English. Avoid slang words, like yeah instead of yes, answering "Huh?" instead of "Excuse me?" "Pardon me" or "I'm sorry. I didn't hear you," which are the more professional ways to respond.

   Another one that sends shivers down my spine is the incorrect pronunciation of the work *ask*, as in "I'll ask her for a raise." Too many people say "ax." Practice pronouncing the word *ask* correctly, even if you have to slow your talking to pronounce it in the appropriate manner.

9. There's nothing wrong with a *hint* of scent to augment your personal style. Notice I said *a hint*. So many people feel they must use cologne and perfume-like substances with wild abandon. It is personally offensive and can even affect people's allergies when the aroma permeates the office area. Countless times I've

had to pull female staff members to the side to ask them to tone down their perfume. I've even witnessed staff spraying their office with Lysol and other similar disinfectants to quickly evaporate the offending smell. It can become painfully clear that you are offending someone in the elevator based on nonverbal expressions, like frowns, covering the nose, a hand waving in front of a face. Don't let yourself become the focus of these expressions.

10. Loud gum chewing or gum popping at your desk or in a meeting is inappropriate.

11. The same goes for loud chewing while eating and talking with your mouth open. Don't become nicknamed "the cow."

12. If music is allowed at your desk, it should be played low enough not to offend others. If you can, earplugs are always wise. Heavy metal and rap and hip hop are never appropriate in the office.

13. No swimsuit calendars of men or women should adorn your personal workspace. Ditto for pictures or calendars of your favorite musical artists. Posters of Art Kelly, Beyoncé, and Tim McGraw should stay at home. Also, make sure you check with your manager or HR manager; there may be written guidelines regarding office space decoration.

14. In the lavatory and break rooms, please remember to clean up and pick up after yourself. No one wants to have to do another's work in this area.

15. Always, always treat your boss with respect. Eye rolling and teeth sucking when you are requested to complete an assignment will speak volumes about your work attitude without you uttering a sound.

16. Interrupting others in a meeting or discounting their opinions is also very disrespectful. Everyone has a right to their opinion, whether or not you agree with it. You can be agreeable in disagreeing by politely saying, for example, "I disagree with you, Jim, and here's how I'd approach this matter."

17. No cursing, yelling, or name calling in the workplace, please!

18. Most professional workplaces have written policies on the appropriate use of e-mail, voice mail, and the Internet. Many workplaces ask new employees to sign that they have read such policies. Make sure you adhere to them to avoid disciplinary action and/or termination. Even if your desk neighbor, Joe, doesn't adhere to the policies, don't let management use you as the first example.

19. If you're given a team assignment, make sure you assume your share of the responsibility for the task assigned to you. If you don't and someone else must complete it, your coworkers will quickly turn on you, and word will spread that you're not a team player.

20. Never gossip about anyone in your workplace. Treat your colleagues with respect. Word quickly spreads, and you'll likely be labeled as the office gossip. Soon they'll be gossiping about you.

21. By now hopefully it's obvious that you will be judged by how you act at an office party and/or function. Losing your shoes, getting drunk, or overly flirting with someone else's spouse, girlfriend, significant other, or even the boss will generate unwanted repercussions at the office on Monday and thereafter.

In sum, you must project the image by which you would like others to perceive you. I've often said that those aspiring to be promotable should always dress and behave up to the next level. Hopefully that's someone who can be modeled appropriately. *Expect* that you will be tested daily based on how you act, interact, dress, and speak, and you will always be prepared.

Communication on the Job

How many more ways and times can it be emphasized that communication is vitally important in any role we assume? *Any* human contact entails some form of communication, and communication affects how people perceive you, which in turn affects what they are willing to do as they work with you.

On the job, the ability to communicate effectively can enhance or detract from one's ability to obtain the appropriate message. If you are not seeking to understand as well as to be understood, how can you expect to secure and maintain any credibility with your staff, your peers, your supervisors, or anyone else, for that matter?

The first important feature to successful communication is that when you are speaking to an individual or a group, whether small, medium, or large, is to take a breath and try to assess the mood of your audience. Believe it or not, people are sending all kinds of communication signals even when they aren't speaking. Are they sitting quietly with hands folded, seeming expressionless? Perhaps they really are content and fully prepared for your presentation. Are their arms folded? Brows furrowed? Eyes squinted? Perhaps a defensive show-me stance? Smiling and arms at rest? Open and willing to hear your every word? Truly the only sure way to know that your assessment is right on is to ask the person sitting quietly with hands folded if your assessment is correct; "You seem to be somewhat content." To the person with furrowed brows, ask, "Do you have a question or concern I can address now?"

These are just two suggestions for how to relax yourself and be open to the communication at hand. Further, as you speak, to understand as well as to be understood look for ways to connect with your audience. Sharing your personal stories as people tell their own, especially in one-on-one sessions, is an opportunity to reveal through your humane and feeling tone that you are indeed able and willing to share experiences, that you're able to connect.

I was recently faced with a situation where I had to change two department heads. One of the current department heads had resigned, and I had to move a current department head from her current role. What made the move problematic was the department head I was moving up had bonded with and was much beloved by her staff. The staff was upset with my decision, feeling that I should move some other department head to the now-vacant role. A flurry of phone calls, anonymous letters, and e-mails expressed their chagrin. I felt it important that I meet with the staff to calm the waters, so to speak, and explain my decision.

I also knew that my credibility was on the line. I had to come across as being earnest about their concerns, even though some of my peers would discount their issues as mere whining. So I went in the next morning carrying donuts, not as a cheap bribe but because eating and talking always seem to relax people a bit. Even so, I could assess that they were still tense and ready to pounce if I misspoke. I opened by explaining I was there to hear their concerns, even though I could determine from their e-mails that they may not agree today with my decision. I asked that they understand it as the best possible outcome with the information I had available to me at the time.

While listening intently, I had to determine what I could give them to turn this situation into a win-win. They sat mostly at the edge of their seats, with arms folded and tense faces, and I did initially feel I was walking into the proverbial lion's den. Question after question followed, outlining their outrage and wonder at why they were being picked on. It was true that this department was in some fiscal difficulty, but I assured them they were not being punished for this. A number of factors, mostly out of their control, had contributed to the need for a department head who could quickly bring fiscal strength and good leadership to this department. The staff began to relax and open up; they indeed had other issues in the past year, prior to my arrival, that they felt had not been addressed. One of them required some flexibility in scheduling. Although scheduling had been under the authority of Human Resources, I determined that I could possibly make a one-time exception due to the current special situation, but I knew that I would also need to communicate with Human Resources so they would not feel their authority had been usurped. In situations like this, faced with an angry staff eager for someone to blame, it would be easy for the person in charge to say, "Yes, whatever you want." It could get me off the hook, yes, but if I couldn't deliver, I'd sacrifice major credibility and lose ground in moving the organization forward.

Thus I told the staff I would check with Human Resources and get back to them with an answer by the end of the day. I researched with the HR department and found that I could have some degree of flexibility based on the special circumstances. I communicated this to the staff's department head so she could be the bearer of good news.

The lesson here is to assess the mood of the audience, explain as much as feasible as honestly as you can, and always try for a win-win.

E-Mail Manners

E-mail is one of the dominant ways of communicating in today's business world. If you want to be viewed as a true professional, your e-mail communications have to be professional.

Here are a few suggestions on how to use e-mail appropriately, although most organizations have already set up guidelines.

1) Just like spoken words and written memos, e-mail cannot be called back. It thus behooves us to ensure we communicate with a sense of respect and courtesy. It is never appropriate to criticize, berate, or use any manner of bad discourse in e-mail.

2) Any e-mail with ethnic, racial, or sexual jokes should always be considered off limits.

3) Try to keep e-mail communiqués as brief as feasible. No one wants to read memos longer than two paragraphs, unless an attachment accompanies it. E-mail is one technology method that should assist, not hinder its users.

4) Remember that once an e-mail is sent, it can't be undone. If you send a communication with negative comments, it's there for all the world to see. It can come back to haunt you or stump your upward mobility even after you leave your present employer, as many professions are well networked.

Organizing Your Work (When the Boss Keeps "Adding It On")

Now that you're in a management position, you'll have more responsibility, and the amount of work can be overwhelming at times. Sometimes, you may find yourself in a situation where the boss drops by midafternoon to add one or two additional assignments just when you've initiated work on the two assignments he gave that morning. Even the most organized person can become frazzled when this occurs. First, take a deep breath, and then exhale slowly. You're a highly valued employee. Obviously, your boss has confidence that you have the skills to complete these assignments. So now you have three more. Evaluate, with your boss's assistance, the deadlines for each assignment and which require the most research and additional resources, and so on. Then it's time for a conversation with the boss to give him your findings so you can both evaluate which of these tasks needs to be completed first. The case study below is an illustration of such a process.

Regina is a recently promoted manager who is trying to make a good impression on her new boss. However, her boss is very demanding, creative, and energetic and keeps coming up with new projects with deadlines that keep getting closer together.

Regina is becoming overwhelmed. She wants to meet her responsibilities but doesn't know which report of the three assigned, which are due on the same date, she should complete first. What should she do?

In the final manuscript I received, the page was messed up & there was no boxing of the case study as above. I assume that in the actual final I'll receive this will be fixed. Thank you.

Regina can first list the projects on a sheet of paper with their due dates. Then she should do her own assessment of the priorities for completion and note her thoughts about why she made project one number one, and so on. After this is completed, she should send the information to her boss, at the same time scheduling a meeting to discuss her list.

She can be assertive yet compliant by stating, "You may not realize it, but you gave me a media project and school projects within the last two weeks, and all are due by September 1. I have the other four projects that are due by Labor Day. I took the liberty of sending you a memo with my own suggestion for how I could prioritize them. If these don't meet with your approval, I'm of course open to your ideas about which of the projects due on September 1 you would like me to complete first."

Regina is proactive by showing her boss she knows she has work to do but is up against multiple deadlines and is seeking to work with her boss to gain consensus on how to schedule the projects appropriately.

TIP = Time Is Personal: Ten Ways to Get Organized Now for Daily Sanity

Because working women have so much on their daily and weekly schedules, I offer these suggestions for how to make life easier for you that give you more time to spend with yourself and family.

1. **TIP:** Time is personal. Realize that unlike money, you can't get time back once it's spent. Even when you spend money, you can probably eventually get some back.

    But time once spent can't be replaced. That's why it's so important to prioritize the time we're going to spend. Whether allocating chosen time for our family, work, or volunteer efforts, spend the minutes wisely. As Benjamin Franklin said, "The years will take care of themselves."

2. **Big Block Calendar**

    Buy a block calendar and put it in the kitchen, which is usually one of the first stops you make within ten to fifteen minutes of arriving at your house. Hang it on the wall. The blocks for each day should be at least three fingers' wide. In my house, I use my own initial and my son Justin's first initial to identify our appointments: Monday, *J—10:00 a.m. crew, E—Toronto p.m.* Wednesday, *Return E, back 7:00 p.m.; J—2:00 p.m. dental appt.* I even use it to schedule happy-birthday calls.

3. **Clothes Scheduling**

   Twenty years ago my friends laughed at me; now they thank me! With our "busy getting ready in the morning" schedules, it is important not to waste time deciding what to wear that day. So, unless I have emergency travel plans, I review my upcoming week's schedule on Sunday afternoon to decide what outfit works best, from a casual dress-down day to a cocktail party. I can determine if I have what I need or if a button is about to fall off or has fallen off without leaving me franticly searching for a replacement. I do the same for the accessories needed for each outfit.

   Once I spent fifteen minutes rehemming a skirt whose lining was coming undone. Can you imagine how potentially late I'd have been if I didn't discover the loosening hem until I was about to walk out the door for work? Yikes!

   Do the same for your children, but let them have a choice of outfits. Always offer children a choice so they can have some right of self-determination also.

4. **Usage Replacement**

   This is handy for restocking everything from toilet paper to eye shadow. If there is enough mayo for one sandwich left in the jar, I always buy one more jar to replace the one I'm about to open in the pantry. This ensures I don't have to run out before I make a buffet portion of potato salad. As soon as the last four rolls of toilet paper are about to be opened, it's time to restock.

   Grocery stores usually have sales at some point between replacement times, and that is another a good time to replace stock. I always use coupons. Why give wealthy product corporations extra money by not cashing in a coupon? Large stock companies, like Sam's Club and BJ's, have come to the rescue of those who want to restock big time and have the storage space to do so.

5. **Clothing Essentials**

   If you don't have at least one week's worth of underwear waiting, you're bound to hear the whine, "I don't have any clean T-shirts." If you're a busy career woman who doesn't have consistent household help, do yourself a favor and buy extra when it's on sale. Kids usually don't outgrow socks and underwear as fast. In the interim, as soon as you feel they're ready start to teach your family member(s) how to do their own laundry.

6. **Meal Planning**

   Learn early to prepare or half-prepare at least one or two other meals during the weekend for the week ahead. Although it sometimes happens that a family member may have a deep craving for something you hadn't planned, it's always good to be flexible no matter what you do. Meat loaf on Saturday can become meatball bombers on Tuesday. Broiled salmon on Sunday becomes salmon quiche on Wednesday.

7. **Work Schedule**

   If you supervise employees, how often do you meet with them? An open-door policy enhances team performance, but you must be careful how you use it or it will detract from your assignment completion.

   I try to leave the first forty-five minutes and last forty-five minutes of the day free for staff to schedule time with me. This was especially helpful on days I traveled and wasn't in, as it allowed time for quick staff briefings.

8. **To-Do List**

   Yes, I use a to-do list—my A list for each day at the office. This should not overwhelm you, however. If it's too long, you'll frustrate yourself if you don't get through the list. But you'll also get some satisfaction by completing those you did.

At the end of each day, start a new list. I use lined yellow four-by-six cards and skip lines so it doesn't look crowded.

For the techno crowd—smartphones can save you from having to manually use pen and paper.

On Friday evening I review the list of items still not crossed off. This is when I reassess the list. Was it really important to complete? Or is it something I'll delegate to my B list to be done later. Of course, emergencies are bound to come up. So don't beat yourself up if you don't get through the A list each week.

9. **Learn to Be Dually Focused**

That is, get two things done at once. While on hold, it's a great time for you to review mail quickly, write checks, or skim quick correspondence. The saying "trying not to read the same mail twice" continues to be quite relevant.

Your secretary can help sort mail that can be read later, like professional journals and upcoming conference and promotional materials. These are great for taking with you to doctors' offices, when you're waiting to pick up your child, and so forth. I always have a few of these in the car for times like that.

Travel time is also a great time to write thank-you notes, quick notes, and notes of congratulations to family and colleagues; keep a small assortment of these at the ready. When I have time between flights at airports, there's bound to be some funky and unique stationery store with a sale, and then it's the time to stock up. Even in line at the car wash I've managed to reduce extracurricular reading.

10. **Time for Yourself!**

Healthy eating, exercise, and proper grooming will help you maintain good physical condition. If you're not healthy and emotionally balanced, you'll be less able to take care of the needs of your family. Never, ever leave the house looking less than your best, for this will surely be the time you'll run into the office gossip, who'll leave you ripe for the next day's break talk. "Yeah, girl, she didn't even have any makeup on, and her hair was a mess." I'm not saying you have to wear a full regalia of foundation and such, but pared-down basics make you look like you made an effort. For me, that's eye shadow, mascara, a bit of blush, lipstick, and earrings. If your hair's not curled, then a cute, funky hat or a headband will dress up your hair. Please—never allow any chipped polish! Remove it rather than have it half-on.

I've been a vegetarian for more than thirty-six years, and it's served me well. But I make sure I'm getting the requisite protein and vitamins. Too much of anything is not good for you. When traveling, I always carry dried fruit and a few nut products for protein to avoid eating junk in the airport. Because the local offerings on long airline flights leave one wanting, I usually bring along a veggie sandwich so I can get a good balanced meal.

Enough rest and scheduling vacation time off for yourself and family will keep you truly fit.

Take time for your spiritual health. If you believe in a higher power, then practice it and meditate with it. If not, learn to meditate about something that brings you peace.

In closing, no one can help you unless you are ready and willing to make the effort for yourself.

Performance Evaluations

It is definitely human nature to be tense around work-performance time. Most people want to know that they are doing their jobs and that, basically, people like to work with them. This time can be uncomfortable for both supervisors and employees. But the process doesn't have to be a horrible one for both parties. Below are some suggestions for how to make the outcome at least fair and respectful, if not pleasant.

1. Ensure there is standardization within the company with respect to how employee evaluations will be handled. Not having standardization can leave the organization vulnerable to legal action.

2. Set the time appropriately. Most managers/leaders I have spoken to try to schedule for as early as feasible in the day. The later in the day the event is scheduled, the more likely it could be subjected to rescheduling due to unforeseen emergencies.

3. Don't try to crowd the day with too many evaluation appointments. Two per day is a guideline, lest you become fatigued.

4. Don't use the evaluation to give the employee any surprises. All employees have the right to have inappropriate behavior brought to their attention when the behavior occurs, not once a year at review time. Use the evaluation as an opportunity to set expectations for the employee and the supervisor. What is it the employee needs from the organization to be successful? Does the employee have a goal that the supervisor can help with? The supervisor? What is it the organization needs from the employee to be successful? Setting concrete, measurable goals can help the employee stay focused through the year.

5. Never personalize the evaluation to set up a contest between one employee and another or yourself and the employee. Never say, "Why can't you be more like Jane or Mark?" or, even more demeaning, "When I had a similar position ..." Expect eyes to roll. This is reminiscent of "When I was a youngster, I had to walk ten miles to school. I didn't have buses or parents to take me."
Remember that an appraisal gives both of you the chance to sit back and look at your working relationship. It should be a comfortable time for both parties. Quality feedback all year goes a long way to creating a comfortable yet honest appraisal that's useful for both parties.

Getting the Best from Meetings

I've yet to meet many people who relish the idea of sitting around in rooms to discuss any subject, no matter how dear to them, if there is no clearly delineated outcome. Most people of influence who have held successful meetings would agree on these minimal guidelines:

1. Have a specific agenda with time lines assigned—review of previous minutes for four minutes, director's report for fifteen minutes, and so on. If the meeting is approaching the finish time and there are still issues to address, you have two options. Ask meeting members for a vote to extend the time, or add another meeting. It's my guess that most would select an extension where feasible as opposed to another meeting.

2. If you as a leader already know what decision needs to be made, be up front about it prior to the meeting. For example, "A decision has been made on the selection of the vendor from the Request for Proposal procedure. The purpose of this meeting is to announce the vendor and to assign tasks to move the process along."

3. Brainstorming is always a useful process but can lengthen a meeting considerably. Why not ask meeting participants for written feedback prior to the meeting? Written memos or e-mail can help the leader categorize and distribute information to participants to speed up the decision process.

4. Allow all to participate. Beware of those who love to hog the spotlight or are disagreeable in their disagreement. It's up to the meeting convener to ensure that the meeting stays on the task at hand.

5. Determine the time of day within your organization that is most conducive to agendas. Often people become less attentive in meetings held immediately after lunch because of sluggish digestive systems.

Getting Along

When you join an organization, you will have to interact with many people. Getting along with your boss, your secretary (if you have one), and your staff is important to your success.

Your Boss

Although this may seem painfully obvious, your first ally in the organization should be your immediate superior, because he or she will determine how far and how fast you climb. Since you, as a woman of color, can expect to be more closely scrutinized than your peers, this is one alliance you should form diplomatically.

For starters, although your boss should recognize you as a member of his team and realize that you are mutually dependent upon each other for the success of your unit, he (my pronoun of choice since men still overwhelmingly represent the upper echelons) may not in actuality treat you as a partner in the enterprise. This is your signal to take the initiative, respectfully asking for a meeting at which you can discuss departmental goals and his expectations for your job performance. It's an excellent opportunity to ask about his managerial style. If he requires a monthly written report, for example, does he prefer a lengthy narrative or an executive summary with lists of accomplishments and statistics? How does he want you to report on a daily basis—in person, by memo, by phone? Are there times he is never to be disturbed and times when you should run, not walk, to bring something to his attention? Also, you might tactfully inquire whether there are any tasks he dislikes that you could take on, on his behalf, such as drafting and presenting the department's annual report to senior management. As time goes on and you prove your worth, this type of in-house volunteerism can very neatly overcome the suspicions of the superior who refuses to delegate.

In dealing with your superior, you may need to curb your desire to operate independently. While independence and the ability to work with a minimum of supervision are usually considered marks of an effective manager, your boss may not see it that way. At least in the beginning, you may have to grin, bear it, and ask his approval at every turn. Irritating as this may be, once you gain his trust, you can almost certainly expect to be given freer rein.

Although your boss may be the type who never wants to hear bad news, you should tell the truth at all times, phrasing it as palatably as possible. An example: "Our sales figures for the second quarter are down by 10 percent. My staff and I, however, have come up with these five specific steps to raise them by 20 percent next quarter." Accentuating the positive can soften the blow considerably and avoids the fatal—and unethical—mistake of falsifying results.

Unfortunately, you cannot assume that your supervisor will be supportive, no matter how talented, diplomatic, and accommodating you are. Many employees may believe that their bosses are on their side, fighting fairly for the good of all in the company, but there are bad managers who distrust their people and who consequently undermine them by withholding support, information, or authority. Should it be your misfortune to find yourself assigned to such a tyrant, you have two alternatives: find a sympathetic ear at the next-higher level or find another job. Sometimes you just can't win. A cautionary tale, however, before you choose the latter option and decide to "tell it like it is" before you leave. Early in my career, I did not get an expected promotion, because my supervisor did not feel I was qualified. Although it was a grave disappointment, I kept my poise and my temper. Years later, the supervisor, who had retired but returned to the job market, came to me looking for employment. As the saying goes, "Be nice to those you meet on the way up, because you never know if you might meet them again on the way down."

Assume your boss is a white male with the confidence that you, a female of any culture, could do the job as a manager and so hired you. Of course, you're grateful and hopefully not overconfident enough to think you can now relax because you got the job. Realize that from day one, you are being tested to see if you do meet the boss's expectations. If you're like me, you also want to meet your own expectations and so will work doubly hard to do so. You and your boss are truly in a delicate dance; he leads, you follow—if this tango is going to look good.

Above all, since your relationship with your boss is already sensitive because of racial and sexual perceptions, you should work doubly hard at it. Only then can you achieve a relationship that is honest and allows each of you to exercise your talents and your own management styles and is geared toward success for you, for him, for your department, and for the organization.

Your Secretary

At work remember to treat all with dignity, regardless of their position. Be advised of the special status of the secretary or administrative assistant. *Secretary* actually means "keeper of the secrets." The position has been demeaned often and used as a stereotype of having less power. But remember, heads of departments in the president's cabinet are titled Secretary of Treasury, Secretary of Commerce, and so on. Secretaries who are part of executive committees and voluntary and corporate boards are aligned with power.

Your secretary is your first line of defense, and, if he/she is a good one, fully capable of furthering your career. Antagonize him/her and you may learn to your sorrow that he/she is capable of hindering it too. What you must do is walk a narrow line between icy distance and overfamiliarity.

To set the proper tone of your relationship, invite her (my choice of pronoun), as you did the other staffers, into your office for a get-acquainted chat. You can then explain how you like to work and what you expect of her, and you can solicit her ideas on ways to make the work flow more smoothly. If she is a veteran of the department and you are not, you will find that she is a gold mine of information. While making it plain that you want to maintain open and honest communication, you should be equally clear that what passes between the two of you is to be kept strictly confidential.

By all means, chat with her when appropriate about innocuous topics—what she plans to do over the weekend, the bargains to be had at a department store sale, a story in the morning paper—but take care what you reveal about your personal life and your private career plans. You both never know where your career might take you.

If you have never had a secretary before, you may be able to make use of certain office protocols that I have found helpful.

1. When telephone calls come into the office, I always ask my secretary to find out who is on the line before transferring the call to me. This allows me to decide whether I will take the call then, later, or never. It also permits her to screen calls from salespeople and complaining clients. Suggest that she ask callers, "Will Ms. _____ know what this call is about?" If, for instance, the caller is a job seeker, I have authorized her to ask for a resume and acknowledge its receipt in writing. I have also advised her to listen sympathetically to consumer complaints, take the name and number, and assure such callers they will receive a prompt written or telephone response.

2. If you are meeting with someone in your office, ask your secretary to hold all calls, unless there is a particularly urgent one or one related to your meeting that you want to take. One would hope that she is sharp enough to know when to break the rules—such as when your boss calls.

3. Make your own phone calls. Few exercises in office one-upmanship are more pointless and more annoying than taking a call from a secretary and being put on hold.

4. It will save time if you have your secretary open and sort your mail. Just let her know from the beginning what she should keep, what she should toss, and how she should prioritize the stack—memos from your boss on top, for example.

5. As a backup to your desk calendar, have your secretary make note of your appointments and office deadlines. Not only will she be able to remind you of important dates, it will be helpful to her to know when you are likely to be out of the office or particularly busy. (Ultimately, of course, any missed deadlines are your responsibility.)

6. Unless she volunteers, it is not your secretary's job to make and serve coffee or to run your personal errands. If she does perform these services, remember to thank her rather than accepting them as your due. Always thank her for a job well done, no matter how small. Remember her with suitable cards and gifts at Christmas, on Secretary's Day, and on her birthday, if birthdays are observed in your office.

7. Make time for her when she has a problem, whether personal or business-related, and try to be flexible if she must leave early on occasion because of child care or family emergencies. Make sure, however, that she does not abuse these kindnesses and that she does not come to regard you as a shoulder to weep on instead of an employer.

Your Staff

As a manager, your most important goal is to encourage, goad, inspire, and motivate by whatever means necessary the best work of which your subordinates are capable. It is a position in which you may in the course of a day be psychologist, magician, mother, and cheerleader. Remember, however, that, like your secretary, your staff can make or break you professionally. The epitaph of many a promising career has been "She can't manage people." Here's a qualifying statement: although I include various scenarios that a woman of color, especially black women, may encounter in the workplace, it is important to note that not everyone is against you as a woman of color. You will find allies at all levels, regardless of race, but it is up to you to learn from them and hone the skills needed to reach your level of success. The black woman manager, as noted previously, faces hurdles in this regard that others do not, and I have outlined briefly some rudimentary strategies for dealing with interpersonal problems.

The scenarios below are not meant to overgeneralize but merely to be taken as considerations. The only and best way to achieve clarity or consensus in a conflict situation may be to have a one-on-one conversation with the individual in question. If that doesn't work, you should ask your supervisor and/or HR department for assistance and recommendations. With the growing diversity of cultures in the workplace, we must all be culturally sensitive to expanding populations of Hispanics, Africans, Burmese, and others too numerous to mention here. But if we embrace the notion that diversity makes us stronger, there will be fewer negative issues to address in the workplace that can impede productivity and company profit.

Black Female Supervising a Black Male: Do not be surprised to encounter resentment if you have black male staff. Although we are taught from childhood to be generally supportive of our race, you should realize that a black man may be a competitor, a situation that further confuses an often tenuous relationship. To deal with this situation, first seek input on decisions to be made: "Don, I need to make some cost cuts in the MIS department. What would you recommend we do first?"

Black Female Supervising a White Male: Because the white male has enjoyed a position of authority over minorities and women for so long, he may find it difficult to take direction from or be held accountable to a black woman. He may continually test your competence and your patience to see how much pressure you can take. He and his cronies may rebel openly. (In one extreme instance, when a black woman was appointed head of a social agency dominated by white males, a portion of the staff broke away to form their own unit rather than accept her supervision.)

The white male worker can sometimes provide your strongest opposition. In general, however, you will usually be able to deal successfully with him when you employ strategies similar to those cited for the black male. If he does become troublesome and you are obliged to report him to your supervisor who is also white, be sure you have documented the facts with times, dates, and places in writing. Otherwise, you may find that you are the one branded a troublemaker.

Black Female Supervising a White Female: If a black woman feels she is on a broken treadmill, she has cause. According to statistics compiled by the Equal Employment Opportunity Commission, fourteen times more white women than black women—944,421 versus 65, held white-collar positions at the end of the last decade. More than ten years later, black women still occupy fewer than 3 percent of all management positions held by women.

These numbers may well explain why the black woman supervisor may face special problems with white female subordinates. The white woman, accustomed to dealing with white supervisors and used to black women only in lesser positions, may be both confused and hostile. She may react to you, her black supervisor, resentfully because you have achieved more than she has, or she may spread rumors that you have used your sexuality to get ahead.

Black Female Supervising a Black Female: Dealing with a black woman when you're the boss can sometimes mean resentment comes into play. The black woman you're supervising may believe she should've gotten the position you now hold, may believe you think you're better than she in some way. She may be just as difficult and twice as painful to cope with as her white cohort. I say "painful" because I am always willing to create an environment that aids the development of black women managers when they show that they are eager to take the initiative. To be repaid with rancor and hostility is indeed hurtful. I hired a black female friend who got demoted for a poor performance evaluation by her white supervisor. She was resentful that I didn't step in to have it overturned so she could receive a merit increase. Unfortunately, the white supervisor had substantial documentation to justify his decision, so I had to support the evaluation that was given by the supervisor. The friendship didn't survive, but I always stay true to the facts.

I should add that when you have the power to hire and fire, you should wield it circumspectly. Eager as you may be to initiate affirmative action, you should not hire solely black women, nor should you hire an unqualified candidate just because she is black and female. This type of favoritism can be perceived by your superiors as reverse discrimination and can only reflect negatively on you.

In Summary

As women we must work at trying to be more supportive of our female peers who work and/or volunteer in the community. As a woman, you don't want to be labeled as someone who undermines other women.

Women tend to form more relationships at work, mixing work and pleasure, socializing during and after work. When one is a supervisor and has to reprimand someone she is both responsible for and also eats lunch with, it can disrupt the workings of an entire team. We've all seen or experienced it at some point in our career.

My example happened at a very early age, and I'm grateful now for the lesson it taught me. I supervised a good friend on a clinical care unit. I had to give her some constructive criticism during her evaluation about her poor charting habits. For those of you familiar with quality control and standards, you know this can affect reimbursement and customer satisfaction. Well, this criticism resulted in her not speaking to me for almost ten years. We did eventually patch things up, but it was a hard lesson that taught me to keep some distance between work and special relationships.

Part 4

How to Go Above and Beyond

Based on my experience and what I have witnessed as an executive coach, in order to be truly successful in any field a manager must have perseverance and be eager to learn. This perseverance comes into play after you don't get the job you applied for; you don't hit the sales target; you miss a deadline. And you may not be an expert in the task your boss has assigned you, but you can seek someone who can help you after you've thoroughly researched the topic.

When you are selected for a management position, you will possess certain important qualities: authority in your field based on knowledge and competence, ability to work with and direct others, good communication skills, intelligence and problem-solving ability, perseverance, inner drive, character, dependability, integrity, and maturity. While these traits are also necessary for entry-level positions, to rise higher in the organization you will need to enhance and refine them.

Attaining the upper levels of management is all about power and establishing power bases with your superiors, your peers, and your subordinates. There are two kinds of power: personal power and position power. If you have the first, people produce for you because they like you and are loyal to you personally. While it's pleasant to be popular with your staff, such popularity is often based on lax supervision, and it can evaporate quickly when you need to make some tough judgment calls, such as deciding who gets laid off during a budget crunch. If you have position power, people work for you willingly because they know your authority is based on professional competence. For my money, this is the most lasting form of power and the one for which you should strive.

Leadership development is ongoing because what you need to be a well-rounded leader isn't found in a seminar on executive leadership. This section talks about leadership, networking, and mentoring, as well as other topics needed for success.

Mental and Spiritual Preparedness for Success

Whatever guide you use—your faith or meditation—you will need something to give you a base to ensure that you are mentally equipped to achieve your destined success. Everything starts with what you believe you can do, so mental awareness is important. If you believe that all life is sacred, that all are created equal, then spirituality or mental fitness can form the basis for a leader's personal goals.

All goals are a series of small steps that need periodic evaluation. Visualize yourself in the position you seek and perhaps evaluate where you are in relation to reaching your dream on your birthday or the start of the new year. When I was completing my doctorate, which seemed very elusive, I began to write "Dr. Ellen Grant," "Dr. Ellen," "Dr. Grant" over and over again every day. Believe it; it worked. I used visualization and documentation to achieve my goals. I've known others who have used similar steps to achieve their goals. Remind yourself that "I can do it because I believe in myself first." Persuade yourself that you will surround yourself with positive thoughts. Positive people will allow your brain chemistry to create positive endorphins to help you.

Sometimes you can find inspiration in other faiths or in writings from famous people. Even though this prayer by St. Francis of Assisi may have its basis in Catholicism, without offending anyone, I feel this has an inspiring message:

Lord, make me an instrument of your peace,
Where there is hatred, let me sow love,
Where there is injury, pardon,
Where there is doubt, faith,
Where there is despair, hope,
Where there is darkness, light,
And where there is sadness, joy.

No matter where you find inspiration, how you handle setbacks reveals a lot about how you will succeed. We all experience setbacks: you lose the sale; don't get the exact bonus amount expected, or a storm closes the airport so you miss a presentation. You can grieve the setback. Have a time-limited pity party and then move on. Playing the victim can keep you away from achieving your goals and enjoying life.

When you're in the middle of the setback it is often hard to think. First, take a deep breath. Instead of trying to fix blame and find the first easy way out, stop and think. Senator Hollings of South Carolina used the phrase "The ox is in the ditch," meaning the ox driver and cart are in the ditch and it will take some help from others to get it out. Quickly analyze what happened. How can you fix it? What can you do to ensure it doesn't happen again? You can make a self-assessment as to whether you have nerves of steel or nerves of rubber. It's been theorized that those who succeed tend to be emotionally stronger, and emotional and mental strength are essential for meeting your goals.

Participative Leadership

I'll now spend some time on leadership, which continues to be a moving target in that it's often difficult to define. We often conjure up images of the military (i.e., General Colin Powell), heads of corporations (Lee Iacocca), perhaps a former sSecretary of sState (Madeline Albright) or a church bBishop. My definition of leadership is "the process of influencing others to secure a goal."

Successful leaders should possess certain traits, such as flexibility, good speaking abilities, and analytical skills. I caution you that having or not having these traits is no guarantee of success or failure, but these traits can aid in leadership effectiveness in some situations. It has also been said that there is a world of difference between those who are managers and those who are leaders, though the best managers are also leaders. Managers are more focused on the short-term objective or task, while leaders must prepare the long-term goal and/or vision. In terms of people relations, the manager's attention is directed to how things get done, while the leader's is directed to what events and decisions mean to participants.

I do not mean to imply that these options apply only to leaders of companies and/or organizations. The leader of a nonprofit or church group may need the same skills to advance his or her purpose. In my opinion, leaders may also use management skills as a part of a block-building process to achieve their main goal. For example, in my previous role as cCommissioner of mMental hHealth, I was expected to select a few goals in each of the five areas of disabilities for the county, setting the vision, so to speak. I also undertook such tasks as completing information requests from clients and monthly data reports.

The skills that the leader and manager must employ are often interchangeable. Some of the skills used at both levels include effective written and verbal communication. Obviously, the leader should have a keener, more polished delivery system of skills, including the interpersonal skills needed to get the best work productivity from your staff.

To take the whole area of leadership one step further, I'll add the dynamic concept of collaboration. Collaboration in leadership is more appropriate as we go into the new millennium, in my opinion. Collaboration means working with others toward a common goal. It means sharing everything, including power or resources. General Electric Kitchen Aid competes for sales by collaborating on demographics as pointed out in the Rosener book (1995). It also means allowing as much participation as possible in the decision making.

Leadership Style

There are different styles of leadership. A demand-and-control style of leading is not conducive in the long term to increased workplace productivity. Bosses who lead by intimidation are negatively defined, labeled, and often hung in effigy.

The most easily embraced style is a participative style of management, wherein employees are encouraged to speak their opinions, have input into decisions, and look to senior management for positive role modeling, is proving to be the design for long-term organizational success.

Managers must realize that they become insignificant without a followership that is willing to work with and for them. Managers can also do well by doing good, by showing their employees that they can, in fact, be caring while reviewing and adhering to the company's business forecast.

One manager I was acquainted with (I'll use the name Martha) was a taskmaster and employed a style I identified in my therapy days as "kind firmness." That is, she had specific expectations for employees on what their job tasks were, and employees signed on for them. She also had no problem with discipline when called for. She allowed employees to be innovative in creating new product lines. She cared about employees' work and home balance, and she even subsidized employees' day care and care for employees caught in the sandwich generation who had parents in their care.

As she did herself, she encouraged community volunteerism and partnering with the Boys and Girls Club, for example. The company's annual retreat not only discusses where the business is headed but also incorporates a section on how the company can add value to the community.

Martha is a leader who knows how to lead by example but also knows that by doing so she is building a caring, competitive-based business with a heart.

We have all questioned what kind of leader we are. I truly feel success and leadership are like a journey. What you should be striving for is high concern for people. In addition, many management and executive coaches are skilled at personal assessment inventories. You may research this further via the Internet if you like at www.internationalcoachfederation.com. I will discuss this further in the "Personal Coach" Section.

Leadership in and of itself is an elusive quality that can be likened to a journey, not a destination. One's ability to interact with it is shaped by one's experiences, mentors, and detractors. In my own anecdotal experience, I've interacted with many leaders, men and women, who seem to share many of these attributes:

1. **A collaborative management style.** These leaders are not afraid of Socratic dialogue. They encourage their staff to offer constructive criticism. In making decisions that impact their followership, they are willing to share the power. As long as the organization succeeds, there is no need to be a "power hog." Such leaders recognize their employees for jobs well done in a way that is sincere and engaging.

2. **A sense of fairness.** Decisions, as well as discipline, are meted out with a keen measure of fairness. There is no air of favoritism among employees.

3. **Self-Development.** Such leaders believe in self-development in that they participate in leadership retreats and/or educational opportunities to maintain a current outlook for redefining their personal vision.

4. **Self-Renewal.** Monk-like retreats and/or family vacations assist these leaders in looking at the world with fresh eyes via maintaining a sense of balance in their life.

5. **A positive self-attitude.** When projected toward their followers, positivity increases confidence levels all around. The glass is indeed half-full.

6. **Fun.** Leaders are not afraid to have fun at work when appropriate or hold themselves out for some self-poking. They are usually the first to the karaoke mike or the tank for dunking at the company picnic or to wear the clown mask at the company's Halloween party.

These successful leaders know they need the assistance of others to be successful. They work hard to engage other workers, whether they are internal to the organization or external (community) leaders.

The Four Ps of Leadership

I have found four main values to fine-tune my leadership skills. They are as follows:

1) Perseverance
2) Piety
3) High principles
4) Positive use of power

Through the positive use of power, it really is up to each of us to reach out to one of us to network, mentor, or fight for women's health services or other needs for our family and neighborhood community. We do this so we can all live happier lives. Only then will our daughters, nieces, and grandchildren be prepared for healthy, stronger future leadership positions in the home, workplace, and community. One of my favorite Bible quotes is from Proverbs, reminding us to "speak up for those who cannot speak for themselves, for the rights of the destitute." This reinforces for me that, as leaders, we should remember to act for the greater common good. You have talents that you may not have even discovered yet, but when you believe you can be successful, you will.

Another exercise for success in participative leadership to think about and consider: pray on it, perceive it, pursue it. Act like you're powerful and powerful things will happen for you. Practice it and it's yours! When I was struggling to get through my PhD and almost stopped (I was single and living by myself at the time and work was pretty stressful), I'd say to myself a few times each day and before I went to sleep, "Dr. Ellen Grant." I did this to keep focused on my goal and because the mind *will* incorporate positive feedback so that you'll automatically begin to act that way. Act successful and you will be successful; act like a depressive and you will be so. Act like the boss and that's yours too, if that's what you want. So in sum, I finished my PhD six months prior to my own deadline.

Everything we're after is relative. Some days we cast the net and come home with the empty pail, goal unmet. But we still have to get up and go fishing each day and try to catch something. Ladies, if that analogy doesn't work for you, think of shopping; some days you find just what you are looking for, other days not. Aha! I "see" a few smiles!

In my therapy with people and clients, attitudes about the therapy itself will often determine how successful the therapy will be. It's all about attitude. Dr. Karl Menninger, the famous psychiatrist, said,

"Attitudes are more important than facts" (2013 WorldofQuotes.com). Yes, I'll repeat that: attitudes are more important than facts! *Any* fact, he says. "Seemingly hopeless, is not as important as your attitude toward that fact. If you start your brain thinking about what you want to accomplish, your brain will change and adapt to help you get there."

There is value to having a positive outlook when one is not well, as opposed to feeling all is "doomed."

An elderly friend of mine once said that one sick person will kill two well ones. That is, a person not handling an illness well, drains not only herself, but also the people struggling around her to maintain their *own* physical and emotional needs. The point is, I don't care if your dog died (of course I'm sorry if this happened), your man left you, and the IRS is after you. Your positive attitude can help you overcome. You know women— plan God laughs. But if you jump off that cliff, taking that risk, expect the net to appear and it will! Here is my example:

My dad was sick; I had to pay the IRS $17,000. I didn't get a contract I expected, and my son's hormones had him acting like he'd been hatched from an alien egg—all in one week. So, after I had attended my "pity party," I turned that into action. First, I prayed, especially for my son. "Lord, change him." Yes, it's true. I did pray, and slowly it happened. I worked with my siblings to get my dad stabilized in a nursing facility when he was diagnosed with dementia. I worked with the IRS to review the initial heart-stopping figure of $17,000, which was eventually cut to less than half, with a pay-back plan I could afford. The contract I didn't get taught me quickly not to spend money before I had it.

I also suggest you try journaling, or writing to yourself each day, as I did, especially when you're blue or feeling you don't know what to do next. Looking back at your written entries can help you determine if you're falling into a pattern. And when you're feeling better, you will better understand yourself. You cannot change where you've been, but you sure can change where you're going.

Leading Your Employees

So many organizations forget that, overall, employees do wish to do a great job for their employer. Unfortunately, there is often a disconnect between the employer's wants and needs and the employee's. Employees need to know that they are in fact achieving what the employer needs them to do and be valued.

As a supervisor and leader, you have the power to impact this. Praise at a staff meeting can let people know how much you value them and inspire them to do more. Take the time to praise employees, even if you are only partway to the organization or team's goal.

I'm reminded of Nelson Mandela, former president of South Africa. When he took over, he could have so easily said, "Now is the time for revenge, to make up for all the past injustices done to so many fellow countrymen." But no; he wanted to make his country great. To do so he knew he would need the help of all the people, and so he worked with the very people who'd imprisoned and enslaved him. And today, South Africa continues to go through a cleansing, a healing, but is no doubt on the road to greatness because of his ability to build a great team! The lesson for your own team organization is that you have got to work with people, your peers, to achieve the mission of completing the work—yes, often under tremendous constraints, but it's a noble cause to provide quality to your customer base.

I have also coined these four Cs that I follow through my professional life:

Conscientiousness about work. I want to present the best I can to the job at hand.

Communication: Whether verbal or written, credibility and accessibility are important facets of a true professional.

Consistency of Collaboration: When I work with my team, my peers, and my internal and external customers, it is incumbent to treat everyone as equally as I can, to leave the impression that everyone has a fair shot at receiving appropriate guidance and assistance.

Commitment: I think of *follow through* and *commitment*, the two being intrinsically linked. It means that once I take on a task, I am committed to follow it through to its completion, unless it's humanly impossible. Committing to any task should initially mean that you've given it more than cursory thought. I, for example, have drawn upon the sincerity of the people who asked me to complete the task. They obviously chose me because I have a value they can align with. I will do the job; commit; follow through after thorough analysis of whether the work can fit into my current task portfolio. So many people say yes to a job and take on an assignment, volunteering without assessing the value of the job within the scope of their entire life. Then, instead of bowing out gracefully when it's clear they can't complete, they will hang on to the title but be a no-show, often leaving the person who made the request of them in a very precarious position, vulnerable to a loss of credibility in the eyes of others.

Good supervisors or leaders should remember they are not in their position to command but to lead with their team's assistance and in this leading to know how to follow. Lao Tsu, a Chinese philosopher, said that in order to lead the people, you have to know how to follow. Many on your team are the true knowledge experts; they often have the information and ideas that can make you successful in your own role as a supervisor/leader.

The word *supervision* speaks of one who is in charge of another. Good supervision should mean an employee receives the expectation for their performance and then is allowed to go out and complete the job. The good supervisor has also determined the amount and type of supervision that his/her employees need.

Some employees need some level of daily supervision, depending on the type of work the employee does. A staff nurse on a medical unit requires, at minimum, daily input with their supervisor. A salesperson, however, may only need to check in with the supervisor after turning in monthly sales reports.

The point to be made about supervision is that it can be a tool of guidance for the employee but can also serve as a measure of what additional resources may be needed by the organization to achieve its goal.

Supervisors should know what level of supervision each of his/her employee needs. Some employees, for whatever reason, may need praise instantly and often and may seek out the supervisor for this. Other employees, in contrast, feel they need the very minimum of supervision. These employees know their jobs, do them, and seek out the supervisor only when they feel they need guidance.

These employees can also be knowledge experts. Knowledge experts are usually in lower or middle-to upper-middle management and know their job extremely well; they are often seen in an informal role as an adviser to upper management. You can be asked to supervise a knowledge expert, or you can be considered one yourself.

Some organizational executives seek these people out when needed but also allow them the flexibility to continue to do their jobs. Executives cannot and should not be experts at every facet of their own job; their span of control and the people they supervise are just too many.

The executive and knowledge expert relationship is one based on mutual respect. The knowledge expert respects the executive and the job he or she is attempting to do for the organization. The executive respects the knowledge expert and what he or she brings to the table by assisting to achieve the mission of the organization.

Surround yourself with people who may have more expertise in a particular area than you may have. You will learn from them, and your team will succeed; one person cannot do everything well. Remember, a CEO may have a chief financial officer (CFO) who has the financial acumen to assist the CEO in ensuring the company is on the right financial track.

As a black female, or female of any culture, you must realize that sometimes you will be held to a higher standard of performance. A white male may be able to use a sports analogy when talking about getting his team to a touchdown. However, if a woman were to use something similar, the feedback from her male peers may be that "she tries too hard to be one of us guys." Being your authentic self while being aware that you may have to work harder to win acceptance is a choice only you can make. Even then, there's no guarantee you will ever win acceptance.

Networks

It is important to collaborate with people of interest to you. This collaboration can be used to expand or guide your personal and/or professional development.

My definition of networking is a "collaboration of ideas among those with similar career or social interests." It means sharing risks; it's anticipated that those in the network will help each other, even if the return on investment is not immediate.

Consider where to network, as well as feasibility. You may need a mentor, and you can find the mentor within your networks. Are you in a professional organization of human resource managers, for example, some of whom are seasoned, with years of experience, who may or may not be a woman or someone from your profession or race but may be leaders in the field you respect? Could you use some professional advice? It's all about developing a relationship. You will have different mentors at different stages of your life. You may naturally disengage with some mentors when your career takes a different path or you move to a new city. I myself have what I call a "mentor board" that consists of a white male, black woman, and white woman. These are people I developed professional relationships with who came into my life at the time when I was changing careers. There is no tried-and-true formula in networking. The main goal is the development of a relationship.

Like a plant, networking requires feeding. It should be watered. Networks should not be used just when the individuals are in need! Networking involves risk taking. Learn to deal with rejection or unkind responses to calls and other communication. All tomato seeds that sprout grow tomatoes! The same applies when making new friends or contacts. You must realize that networking does indeed take work! Also, don't assume the worst if a contact is somewhat gruff after being approached by you. A person may be dealing with a family illness or their own career issue. You can always approach contacts again later.

Women often fail to network with women's groups for fear of ridicule and/or rejection from men ("They're getting together to plot," or "They're not serious about their careers.") If you're paranoid, meet outside of work and keep it confidential. You're doing this for yourself, not someone else.

How-Tos of Networking

- First, know yourself. This may require trial and error in determining whom to network with. Also, remember to mix corporate and not-for-profit options.
- Look for connections with people (like the vice president at CBS and vice president at Eli Lilly). Some in your network could become mentors.

- Because women (especially minority women in corporate cultures) may be viewed as outsiders, expect that you may have to make the first move in forming relationships.
- Believe that you belong because you have credentials.
- Choose/develop a variety of networks. Your social network may not include the same people as your professional network. Church members, don't forget, are helpful too. They provide the safety valve of support.
- Don't internalize negativity, even if you are on the team but not in the game (i.e., not given the best-choice assignment.) Make a habit of excellence on the job you have, and you will eventually get your chance. If not, at least you'll hopefully know when to move on for other opportunities.
- Yes, you may be different, (i.e., color, sex), so use it to your advantage. While others are figuring out what part of a stereotype you may fit, you'll be near the finish line.
- Someone helped you. If they didn't you may have never gotten your start in your career. Think more recently of specific instances in your own circle when others have assisted others to be successful; for example, Oprah helped Dr. Phil secure his own successful television show.

I find it bad manners to merely attend a program, say hello by way of introduction, and pass out business cards. The receivers of your card are *not* going to give you a job because you gave them a card. It's important to establish a relationship first, and this is not going to happen during a two-minute conversation at a cocktail party.

I would suggest as a next step after the conversation that you follow up the person with an e-mail or telephone call saying you wish to meet and come to an agreement on what your goal is: "Hi, Mary. It was nice to meet you a couple of days ago at our First Friday reception. As I indicated, I'm interested in seeking your advice on opportunities in the public relations business. I'd like to e-mail you my resume and then set up a follow-up meeting within the next month as accommodates your schedule." This brief approach is a way to establish a true relationship with a person you may choose to emulate.

Mentoring

In my opinion, the mentoring relationship is an active, evolutionary process. It is not merely passed from mentor to mentee. It should be a dynamic, mutually agreeable process where two parties engage in an ongoing exchange of ideas to assist in each other's self-development. Yes, mentors can still learn from taking a mentee. In the best of these relationships, two parties learn and grow from each other.

Your Role as a Mentor

It is necessary to explore this relationship, I feel, because many administrators may feel their management staff are naturals at this when they assign them to oversee junior staff. In fact, if guidelines and expectations aren't made clear to both mentor and mentee, the relationship can be less than satisfactory.

If you are to be a mentor in an organization:

First, the organization must define its own goals in relation to staff development.

- First and foremost, does it embrace the concept of mentoring?
- Is it just to develop staff?
- To orient staff to their job?
- To prepare them for career moves?
- Others?
- Does the mentoring philosophy of the organization emphasize accountability, both on the part of the mentor and mentee?

I also feel it is extremely important as you move in your own career to mentor others. Right now I am mentoring a few young women. One is an insurance up-and-comer in another state who continues to surprise her superiors with her maturity and willingness to take on added responsibility.

While you will not be a mentor for everyone on your team, you should provide and encourage training opportunities for your staff. If you are fortunate, you will have funds or facilities for in-service staff training.

Another plus is a budget that allows you to establish a resource library. Even $200 spent judiciously can allow you to stock videos, used and new books, and publications for staff eager for self-development. You could even form a small committee after canvassing staff for reading recommendations. Even if you don't have funds you can at least keep your people informed of work-related classes by posting schedules and distributing brochures. They will appreciate the interest you take. One quote I'll always remember is that people can be motivated to be good not by telling them that hell is a place where they will burn but by telling them it is an unending committee meeting. On Judgment Day the Lord will divide people by telling those on His right hand to enter His Kingdom, and those on His left to break into small groups. (Rev. Robert Kennedy, quoted in the *Boston Globe,* 1978.)

Other winning approaches to providing mentoring are:

- Granting favors when you can, such as allowing time off for family emergencies or willingly signing for an educational leave of absence.
- Setting a good example for them to follow. When you strive to be the best you can be in your work, when you dress professionally, when you put in extra hours, you become a respected role model for those you supervise.
- Correcting with kindness, directing with compassion. Leadership is built on mutual trust and respect. Intimidation has no place in this relationship. While a cowed and fearful staff may snap to do your bidding at the moment, they will soon either escape or rebel, and the turnover in your department will win you no friends in the executive suite. One quagmire where you must tread delicately to retain your staff's good will is evaluating performance and

correcting when necessary. When you must criticize a subordinate, always do so privately, constructively, and specifically. An example: "Don, I can't accept the report you submitted because you omitted three months of admissions data for 1981. Please amend it and resubmit it to me by Friday. And try to be more thorough next time, won't you?" Don't scream, "You idiot! You stupidly left out three months of admission data for 1981! I want you to fix it even if you have to stay here all night!"

• Using power judiciously. Tempting though it may be to take revenge on subordinates who challenge your authority, don't do it! It could come back to haunt you.

Your Role as a Mentee

The employee being mentored has responsibilities also. It is not one of merely taking/receiving from the person who's been assigned to assist your own development. It is your responsibility to help in the development of your own (career) goals, what you believe can help you improve and advance.

Suzette serves as a middle manager in a health care organization and reports to a director. She is responsible for the lab assistant area and has four lab supervisors reporting to her. She requested a mentor from the company administration to assist her in determining where she wanted to go within the organization promotionally or if, in fact, she wanted to go back to direct patient care as a nurse. She was unsure, however, whether she needed to enhance her management skills, having had no formal training. She felt that a mentor could assist her in this area. She was assigned to be mentored by Jean, a director from another department who had volunteered to be a mentor as much as possible for the organization. Suzette and Jean met and established some mutual expectations.

Suzette advised Jean of her career goals. Jean planned to meet with Suzette for thirty minutes for approximately six weeks. (Bob, Suzette's supervisor, is very supportive of Jean's role as a mentor to Suzette.) Suzette would be given suggestions by Jean on how to define herself within the company.

Personal Coaching

Do you need a personal trainer for your mind, body, and soul? Are you struggling with a lifestyle change—divorce, career switch—or in need of assistance to prepare for your next job promotion? Then a personal coach may be what you need.

A relatively recent phenomenon, since the 1980s coaching has developed into an organized profession. One organization, the International Coach Federation, has thousands of members worldwide. Expertise of its membership expands across a broad range, business to self-development.

Coaching can be viewed as having its roots in organizational development. It is not just consulting, in that consulting deals with improving processes structures and the overall mission of an organization and the players' roles in it. Coaching is more customer-focused, assisting individual and/or groups of people to be more effective resources. For individuals, it is custom-designed to meet their needs.

My definition of coaching is "a process that enhances one's ability to achieve the desired results." Coaching differs from therapy. Coaching is action focused. Therapy is usually focused on emotional healing. Coaches help individuals design their lives in partnership with their client. Coaches can have backgrounds in business; clinical and/or consulting among others.

How can coaching impact your life? Consider the concept of change. Structure, like it or not, brings order to our lives. Everything, from expecting that your husband will be home by seven for dinner or relying on a weekly paycheck, allows us to live our lives in a more disciplined manner. When something happens to disrupt this discipline, we call it change. This change can be traumatic to our emotional, physical, and spiritual health, as well as our general family order.

Change brings the known and unknown to us. A husband leaves, a job is lost, a pet dies—we shift from continuity to dysfunction if we cannot deal with the negativity that change brings. It is important to realize that change can also be positive, like a pay raise; which usually brings more spending flexibility.

In helping you deal with time management, for example, as a coach it's my job to help you deal with how to use it in a positive and more productive manner to make your life easier and/or more manageable. In contrast, its misuse can have a negative impact on your goal achievement. Some call coaches "change agents" who help clients deal with change in a positive manner. A coach is an unbiased, empathic party who will give you honest feedback while engaging in active listening. Specialties run the gamut. A business coach would be appropriate for someone hoping to grow her business; a self-development coach, for example, might suit the man who wants to improve his interpersonal communication skills and thus his potential for promotion within the company. There is a coach for just about any life goal you're attempting to reach.

Regardless of the goal, any coach should go through some basic steps with you in preparation for the coaching assignment. After the coachee relates her background and current history or story, she is asked why she desires coaching; why now? What is she trying to achieve through coaching? What timetable is anticipated? After the coach covers her own credentials and costs, usually a verbal agreement backed up sometimes with a written contract is made. I, for example, need a minimum of three sessions for each potential client or coachee to assess their needs via a written self-assessment and/or other assessment instruments. The sessions can be completed in person, over the telephone, and/or by e-mail. Often, "homework assignments" are given to the coachee for working through issues that are leaving the client dissatisfied and/or unfulfilled.

At the end of each session, it is appropriate for the coach to ask the client, "How do you think you did today? Did you accomplish what you needed to?" Likewise, the coach should strive for some feedback from the client to determine if any adjustments in the contract need to be made: "Is there anything you need from me at present? Do you have any questions or concerns about how our session went today?"

Most people as they approach coaching usually know what they need and are usually quite creative in thinking through how they'd like to live their lives. They just may need a bit of assistance in uncovering the information.

A few questions to ask yourself as you evaluate whether to engage in a coaching relationship include the following:

- Am I truly happy in my present situation?
- Do I want the change for the right reason? (More job satisfaction? Do I just want a new job because my sister-in-law got one?
- What would my best world look like and what do I need to change?
- I know I need to change my behavior in order to receive this promotion, but I think I need help.

These might be areas a coach can assist with. A good coach will work holistically with the total person to help achieve true life balance.

Your Health

Becoming a leader and a supervisor means taking on increasing areas of responsibility, and it is easy to not make your health needs a priority. How many of you take a mall walk or daily walk around the block? Good for you! Exercise can alleviate some of that stress. An AOL report by Pam Kruger cited a report by the American Psychological Association that said women earn 77 percent of what men make. Women are more likely than men (28 percent versus 20 percent) to report having a great deal of stress (8, 9, or 10 on a 10-point scale) (APA Press Release [January 2012]).

You've heard of the type A personality that tries to do two things at once, like finishing other people's sentences while attempting to hold a meeting. Well, a term attributed to women that I learned recently is the type E personality. She is the career woman who tries to be Everything for everybody. Another more recent term is the quad-A type—four times the type A.

We work so hard at our jobs and then as wives and mothers in our communities that we have no time for ourselves. Unfortunately, women are now catching up with men interms of heart attacks and other coronary conditions. According to the American Heart Association website Facts about Heart Disease in Women, "Heart disease is the No. 1 killer of women, causing 1 in 3 deaths each year; that's approximately one woman every minute." In the near future, not only will we gain pay equity but also the same rate of disease that men do, which go along with work and success. We women have a slight edge, on average outliving men by seven years, as you probably know. This is one edge that I would like to maintain! One of the lessons I learned early on was to take a mind break to empty my mind of negative thoughts and negative energy for just five minutes midway during the work day (and just before going to sleep). You'll be refreshed and ready to take on the rest of your day.

One trick I used was to use a five-minute sand timer. I would turn it upside down and concentrate on the sand pouring from one section to the next, the negative into the positive. I just concentrated on emptying my mind and relaxing. After a while, especially at night, you can achieve the same thing by visualizing the negative energy flowing out and positive energy replacing it.

If you don't have a timer handy, you can just pour water from one cup to another. My point is to take charge of your life so you don't overstock yourself with negative energy. It can deplete your state of wellness, decrease your effectiveness and productivity, and ultimately not allow you to reach your goal, whatever it is.

There is indeed a strong mind/body connection. Did you know that negativity can be responsible for people not healing well after surgery? "Researchers have linked dozens of physical symptoms to stress overload, from fatigue to weight gain" (Editors, *Prevention*, "Is Stress Messing with Your Blood Sugar," November 3, 2011). It's also important to take a walk outside at some point during your day, besides walking to your car in the morning. Natural light is a vitamin and helps keep mood stable, especially in the winter, when we're less inclined to go outside at all. If you are in a windowless office, you are not helping your body to maintain normal functioning if you don't get enough natural vitamins contained in natural light sources. I know it's even harder for career moms to fit in some natural-light time due to busy schedules. However, a brief period of natural light is a pure vitamin.

I don't believe we're able to turn work off the minute we get home, especially if we've had a bad day. There could possibly be some aftershocks in your home life. Also, keep in mind that a recent study showed that working mothers spend an average of forty-four hours on the job and thirty-one hours on family responsibilities. The major breadwinner in a family generally spends less time on household chores than the lesser breadwinner.

Traditional organizations have a tendency to be very paternalistic and, to use one of my therapy terms, foster a culture of codependency. By *paternalistic*, I mean a concept where the parent or boss is in charge, with limited delegation and decision making. Goals and rules come from the top and are expected to be followed.

I relate the fostering of a culture of codependency to the adult child of an alcoholic parent. The adult in her codependency sees no value in her life. She, for example, sees value only in the environment. That is, she sees value in her title at work, as the mother of her children, but stripped naked before God she does not know who she is. She wanders about, seeking instant approval, gets the next promotion, and does not know how to experience satisfaction. *Unless* she is unhappy, she is in control of everyone in her life. "I know what's best for you; you don't have to think for yourself. I'll do your thinking for you" is the theme of her life at work, at home, and in her relationship with her children. So many things (health, work, lovers) are not within our control or our power. To seek to validate yourself only through them is to run the risk of truly not having peace with yourself.

In Conclusion

My aim, as I explained at the beginning, is to create an environment where the woman or woman of color can receive her due in her profession and take her rightful place in the ranks of management. If you are a woman who dares to have that dream, you already know that creating such an environment is definitely not a do-it-yourself project. There will never be an end to the hard work you will need to do to carve your career niche. There will never come a time when there is no more to learn. There is no absolute assurance that you will always land the perfect job and receive every cent of salary you're worth.

It is my hope that we as a nation will be able to capitalize better and further on the commonalities among us.

It is also my hope that companies and employees will reduce the loud, resonating chorus of differences down to barely audible whispers. Let's work on embracing not only the diversity of our heritage but also diversity of thought.

We will once and for all recognize the value that each individual brings to the workplace so that productivity, profit, and respect will be common threads for all involved there.

Appendix

As a manager and a leader, you will encounter many different types of people. I've included this list of situations, as well as proposed solutions, to help you see how they might be managed.

(Please, always consult your own company's Policy and Procedure Manual and consult with your human resources expert to ensure the advice offered is in keeping with their guidelines before proceeding to action.)

Management Skills Review

1. The Supervisor Who Flouts the Rules
    Your colleague, Sheila Shine, lets her staff take half-hour morning and afternoon breaks instead of the fifteen-minute rest periods company policy allows. Your staff wants to know why they can't take thirty minutes too. What do you tell them and what do you do?
    First, while you may agree that it's unfair for the other unit's workers to take longer breaks, you should tell your staff that you expect them to obey the rules in your department and that you appreciate the fact that they do. Avoid criticizing Sheila in their hearing, however.
    If your staff continues to grumble, take the matter up with Sheila directly. Ask whether she's aware that her staffers are taking twice as much break time as permitted. (She may not be; she may not be as familiar with policy as you are.) Ask her help in following the

rules, thereby presenting a united front to your respective staffs. If she continues to allow long breaks, suggest that you and she meet with your joint supervisor and ask for your superior's ruling on the matter.

2. The Supervisor Who Shows Favoritism

   Pat Pauly has recently been appointed chairperson of the Nursing Department at Manila College. Pat has been friendly for many years with Sue Smith, one of the department's secretaries. You, as college dean and Pat's superior, advised her when she was promoted that in her new capacity she could no longer fraternize with her staff if she hoped to supervise them effectively and impartially. Pat agreed and said she would treat Sue no differently than the other secretaries. Now, however, you hear that Sue is getting special treatment, such as taking days off without going through channels like everyone else. What do you do?

   Ask Pat whether what you hear is true. If she denies it, remind her that people may misinterpret her friendship with Sue as playing favorites; then continue to monitor the situation. If Pat confirms that she has given Sue special privileges, let her know that you are displeased and warn her that she can be demoted if she continues to put friendship ahead of her responsibilities.

3. The Supervisor with the Big Mouth

   Jan Hansel, who reports to you, supervises ten production line workers. You have occasionally heard Jan harshly criticizing one or more of the workers in a loud tone of voice that everyone on the line could hear. What do you do?

   Set a good example. Arrange to speak with Jan privately and ask her whether she's aware that her voice carries and that her tough, often unjustified, criticism is wreaking havoc with the entire unit's morale. Remind her that every worker, regardless of status, is entitled to respect, suggest that she take people aside when she must find fault, and urge her to make constructive comments. If you can, recommend that she take an in-house training seminar on supervisory skills.

4. The Suspected Alcoholic Employee

Jim Jones, a clinical nurse specialist, has been with the Boston Health Maintenance Organization—of which you are director—for six years. Lately, you have noticed that he is spending less time with his primary patients; he frequently drops and breaks supplies; he often comes in late or has his wife call to say he's sick. What's more, in the mornings, you suspect you smell alcohol on his breath. You have heard he has family problems. What do you do? Invite Jim into your office for a discussion of his performance. Tell him what you have seen and ask how he intends to improve. You need not—and indeed should not—raise the subject of alcohol abuse, but you might sympathetically ask whether he is having problems at work or elsewhere that are affecting his relationships with his patients. If Jim denies he's having problems of any sort, ask him to explain why his work has not been up to par. Obviously, if Jim admits he has a drinking problem, you should take steps to help him, possibly through the Employee Assistance Program (EAP) or Alcoholics Anonymous. If, however, he does not admit to having a problem, you may have to take stronger measures. For example, if he comes to work noticeably intoxicated, you should send him to a hospital emergency room for a Breathalyzer test or send him home. You should also insist that he seek treatment. Work with him and your human resources department to develop an action plan.

5. The Praise-Seeking Employee

Wes Winston has been a nurse at the Children's Center for three years. During that time, he has complained to you and to other supervisors that he never gets as much credit for all his hard work as everyone else does. What do you tell him?

Take Wes to lunch or into the center's cafeteria for a cup of coffee, making sure that you pick up the tab. While you're chatting, let Wes know that you appreciate his work, mentioning one or two specific tasks that he did well. At the same time, suggest that he could do an even better job—and be recognized for it—if he concentrated on doing the work and worked with his fellow nurses rather than competing with them.

6. The Employee with Physical Problems

   Angelo Augina, an employee with seven years' seniority, has recently returned to work after suffering a heart attack. His doctor has cautioned him, and Angelo has told you that he will have to modify his physical activities indefinitely. What should you do?

   You have two alternatives: (1) you can assign Angelo to his old job but alter the work load so that he does not overtax himself, or (2) you find (or create) another, less demanding, position that will allow Angelo to continue working and will also benefit the organization. Either course would be appropriate for a faithful employee who wants to work. If he wishes to know more about his options, you might discuss your firm's provisions for disability retirement, but be sure to do so in such a way that he will not feel that you are pushing him or that he is unwelcome to return to work.

7. The Unethical Employee

   As head of an insurance agency, you require your staff to submit quarterly sales reports. You learn, however, that Mary Marks, one of your top sales executives, has used inflated figures in her report to win the quarterly sales award. In the past, Mary has done a great deal for your company. What do you do?

   You should evaluate this employee's termination from the organization. Her lack of ethics may hurt your agency more in the long run than losing her skills as a salesperson will in the short term.

8. The Victimized Subordinate

   You are the assistant to a vice president in a large public relations firm. Your boss, Mr. DePiro, encourages you to talk about your ideas for various projects with him. "Brainstorming," he calls it, or "bouncing ideas off each other," but you have now learned that he has passed some of your best and brightest ideas on to senior management as his own. What do you do?

   There's not much you can about Mr. DePiro's past theft of ideas, but in the future, put your ideas in a dated memo and, if appropriate, copy other staffers so that your authorship is protected.

9. Inappropriate Behavior

   Michael was considered an excellent supervisor in the IT department of a large technology company. He was talented; a number of innovations were attributed to his leadership. He was also helpful to those who requested his assistance. Michael, like all employees, had signed the organization's code of ethics agreement prohibiting use of the Internet to access pornographic sites. He had already received one verbal and one written warning from his supervisor, John. However on Friday, when John was off, it was reported to Mary, next in charge, that Michael had again been to a porn site. She did not witness this herself. Is she still obligated to take some disciplinary action?

   Yes, Mary is still obligated to bring this immediately to Michael's attention. Further, this inappropriate behavior could probably be confirmed via the company's mainframe station, which had been put on alert regarding Michael's disagreeable behavior. Mary should consult with the company's human resources department to determine the most decisive, legal, and appropriate action.

10. The Idea Thief

    Julie attends the weekly management team meetings with her peers. She is assertive and self-motivated. However, when she presents her ideas, often it does not appear she is heard or responded to by

Mike, her vice president—until she hears her contributions later in the same meeting presented to the team by Mike. Julie has become quite frustrated. What advice would you give her?

If the idea was the result of an assignment given to the team—that is, the team members were to return to next week's meetings with suggestions on how to increase sales for the next quarter—Julie should present her conclusions in writing with her name on it.

If it is a random discussion and she hears Mike take her idea to have the advertising department come up with a coupon offer in next week's newspaper, Julie could respond this way: "Mike, thanks for reinforcing my earlier recommendation to have the advertising department develop the coupon. I do appreciate your support. How soon should I proceed to set up the meeting to discuss this?"

In public and diplomatically, Julie has taken the initiative to reinforce her own leadership skills.

11. We're *All* Tired! Working Mom vs. Stay-at-Home Mom

Maria is an attorney, the single working mom of Brandon, age seven. Since her divorce, she has not been able to consistently take her turn in the neighborhood carpool; she must leave home at the same time as the carpool to get to work. Marti, who is the stay-at-home mom of Kelly, age seven, and Ben, age five, feels Maria is not doing her share of driving and confronts Maria about this one day in the driveway.

Marti: "You know, Maria, I've had to cover for you at least four times in the past two weeks for carpool. You're never available!"

What should Maria's response be?

"I realize this, Marti, and appreciate your help. My boss expects me to be in on time, and as I'm still on probation as a new employee, I'm trying to keep up."

In addition to this initial response to Marti, Maria could also offer something in return to assist Marti, such as having Kelly and Ben come to Maria's house on Saturday for a playdate. This gives Marti some time for herself and shows Marti that Maria understands quid pro quo. Maria could also offer to make a casserole one night a week to assist Marti with dinner duties. The point is that working moms don't always have the same home assignments as stay-at-home moms, but they can be supportive of each other in various ways.

These are just a few of the possible supervisory situations you will encounter during your career. Always consult your human resources department for appropriate policies and procedures. In general, however, you will gain the respect of your superiors and employees alike if you observe these five Golden Rules of Management:

1. Respect your fellow man and woman, keeping in mind that each person is unique. Show your respect by criticizing the action, not the person. Be careful of your language, avoiding profanity and belittling remarks at all times. Never hit or physically abuse an employee.

2. Set fair and consistent standards for all employees. The good boss, and that's what a successful manager is, never shows favoritism.

3. Listen. Good communication is the key to effective management.

4. Keep employee confidences; it's the one sure way to gain their loyalty and trust.

5. Literally, do unto others as you would have them do unto you. Join them at staff parties, and pitch in when deadlines loom. Let them know they can count on you in good times and bad. Look out for your staff, and, above all, encourage and reward good performance whenever you can.

I've presented much advice gleaned from my own experience and other sources. Ultimately, you must be comfortable in your own skin. No amount of counseling or advice from authors will help you succeed if you aren't open to receiving constructive feedback. Exude the confidence to know you deserve to be at the management table.

BIBLIOGRAPHY

Bureau of Labor Statistics. "Table 1: Employed and Experienced Unemployed Persons Detailed by Occupation, Sex, Race, and Hispanic or Latino Ethnicity, 2012." Annual Averages 2012. Unpublished Tabulations, January 2013. www.bls.org.

Eagan, Matt. "Leading Women Still Missing: Female Business Leaders." *CNN Money*, March 24, 2015.

Jackson, M. "Corporate Racism Persists Despite Diversity Programs." *Buffalo News*, 1996.

Maslow, A. H. *Toward a Psychology of Being*. New York: Harper and Row Publishing, 1962.

Rosener, Judy B. *America's Competitive Secret—Woman Managers*. New York: Oxford University Press, 1995.

US Department of Health and Human Services, Centers for Disease Control and Prevention, National Center for Health Statistics NCHS Data Brief. No. 125, July 2013.

Wynter, Leone E. "Study Measures Status of Female Managers." *Wall Street Journal*, 1997.

Printed in the United States
By Bookmasters